The Art of Oboe Playing

by Robert Sprenkle

Including
Problems and Techniques of Oboe Reedmaking
by David Ledet

Illustrations by Karl Kneisel

© 1961 by Summy-Birchard Music
division of Summy-Birchard Inc.
All rights reserved. Printed in U.S.A.
ISBN 0-87487-040-2
3 4 5 6 7 8 9 10 11 12 13 14

Summy-Birchard Inc.
exclusively distributed by
Warner Bros. Publications Inc.
265 Secaucus Road
Secaucus, New Jersey 07096-2037

Contents

Introduction

The *Art of Oboe Playing* is an attempt to illuminate and to help solve some of the problems that confront oboists and their teachers. The principal points of discussion are "how" and "why" various factors contribute to or interfere with effective playing. Excellence in musical performance is limited not only by one's lack of mastery of the instrument, but also by one's lack of capacity to project creatively the ideas and the spirit of the music before it is played. We cannot hope to *exceed* our concept of what is required. At times we must even expect to *fall short of* that goal. We, as performers, actually undertake two parallel endeavors: (1) consciously to seek to know and understand music, and (2) to cultivate the instrumental technique necessary to bring our musical ideal to reality.

Aesthetic satisfaction is the goal of any musical endeavor. Players and teachers share an obligation to search out the best means of achieving this satisfaction without undue concession to convention, expediency, or haphazard instinct. We should certainly utilize the resources of science available to us because creative and sensitive musicianship deserves the most fluent, reliable, and undistorted medium for its fulfillment. Musical results are all-important, but we are more likely to achieve and maintain a consistently high level of performance if our efforts conform with, rather than defy, natural laws.

It would be ideal if all aspiring oboists could study with a fine oboe player, since imitation of a qualified teacher is natural and desirable. An expert teacher-player can furnish proper perspective for the student, pace his progress, lend encouragement and enthusiasm, and, above all, set a good example by his own playing. Often, however, a qualified teacher is unavailable and other sources of information and inspiration must be sought. Method books, recordings, pictures, radio and television all play a part in musical development. A great deal can be learned by listening objectively to the playing of others—not for the sake of imitation, necessarily, but for the sake of more clearly delineating our own ideas. We must resist the temptation to find fault with other performers in order to build our own ego. Faultfinding, which is especially widespread among students, is dangerous because it tends to obliterate the praiseworthy features which are present. Performing musically is a creative process that requires a *positive* attitude, not a negative one. It is better to make an earnest attempt and fail than to refuse to try for fear of criticism.

The *Art of Oboe Playing* cannot substitute for a teacher, but it can give supplementary instruction. It is based on the assumption that the complex, highly co-ordinated, but largely mechanical acts of instrumental performance can best be improved by reducing them to their simplest components and then improving the efficiency of each component act. To do this, we must develop an objective, critical attitude toward ourselves. If careful observation discloses defects in our playing, we must have the necessary perspective to deal with their *causes* instead of merely correcting their *effects*.

Some of the ideas presented may seem strange or controversial, but for the most part they have been derived from two basic premises: that a sustained, undistorted quality of tone is simple and desirable and that the means for control of the instrument must be compatible with good tone production. In other words, the controls should not interfere with or inhibit, but rather should strengthen and reinforce, the way the tone is produced and felt.

The Concept of Learning

Habit is defined as "a disposition or tendency constantly shown to act in a certain way, especially such a disposition acquired by frequent repetition of an act."

Musical performance must, by necessity, be largely habitual because it is so complex and highly organized. Even playing the simplest passages requires literally hundreds of separate habitual acts. Constant use makes an act more fluent and therefore more useful, but since habits themselves are completely undiscriminating, only intelligent listening and practicing can provide the process of selection necessary for improvement. In a given performance situation, our attention must be free to concentrate on balance, intonation, ensemble, and other spontaneous and creative details. Therefore, the *means* whereby we accomplish these ends must become automatic. Our subconscious habits and reflexes provide our technique. It is unfortunate that the very process of learning a thing well enough to do it fluently tends to remove it from the level of critical consciousness. This is why our playing habits tend to escape judgment, and why good, bad, and indifferent habits are perpetuated with equal tenacity.

Most of us start out without much musical background and learn music at the same time that we are learning to play the oboe. The desire to perform disposes us to reach that end as quickly as possible. Under these conditions it is unlikely that we will have enough patience to give the proper importance to basic playing techniques even if we are made aware of them. This, of course, is another reason why a good teacher is so important.

To improve, we need to know not only how we want to sound (which involves projecting the mind's conception at least a few notes ahead), but also how we can best achieve that result. Only then can we see the disparity between what we were doing and what we *thought* we were doing. This is difficult because the same instincts which help form our habits hinder our judgment when we try to change them.

Our biggest asset is that we can slow down the sequence of events and devote our attention to the various elements long enough to evaluate their functioning critically. In this way we retain the flow of continuity while we make the necessary changes in individual habits. It is important to perform the act slowly in order to think through the solution needed to correct an error. This method is easily applied to wrong notes, rhythms, etc., but its application to more basic playing habits is not as simple. In the incorrect use of the embouchure, for example, or the incorrect position or action of the tongue, or a failure to provide adequate breath support, it is helpful not only to slow down the processes, but also to simplify them. The various performing functions should be thought out in a logical sequence and put into action. Controls are then added without interrupting the basic tone production and feeling. The order in which these performing functions should be considered is:

1. Posture
2. Embouchure (position of tongue, lips, and reed)
3. Supported breath pressure
4. Control with lips
5. Control with tongue and fingers
6. Vibrato

Because of their elementary character, the first steps do not receive the continued attention they require and deserve. Unfortunately, also, any defects in the first steps will hinder the later steps. Therefore, the most basic principles should neither be hurried over nor be relegated completely to the subconscious.

To achieve the maximum use of our physical and mental powers, we should first understand what is required, then learn how it may be obtained, and finally isolate, condition, and strengthen the conscious control of playing functions until the control prevails even under adverse conditions.

We should study the individual functions of playing an instrument one by one, with sufficient time devoted to each one to establish the habit patterns we desire. Each new step is added while continuing control of the previous step or steps, making whatever adjustments are necessary before going on. Each control can and should *supplement* rather than *distort* the others. The result will be a unified feel of mastery of the instrument. Cultivation of a technique based on this approach will enable us to cope with musical problems of all kinds because we will be flexible and reliable in our responses.

With good posture, correct embouchure can be determined and related to it. After that, the proper abdominal support will provide a solid foundation for easy blowing. This is all that should be attempted at first. Later, the controlled use of the tongue, lips, and fingers should be added one step at a time, always maintaining the previously cultivated conditions and feelings. We need a long-range perspective to be successful in this approach to playing. It takes patience and time to apply principles which at first may seem to have an adverse effect on our efforts to play. Only a long view can provide the necessary faith and endurance.

Selecting an Instrument

Choosing a suitable instrument is not a simple matter. There are a number of hazards even when cost is not a factor. Ideally, a prospective purchaser should have a qualified performer try the instrument under actual playing conditions. After a general evaluation of the workmanship and quality of the wood, keys, and pads has been made, special attention should be given to the following:

1. Quality of tone
2. General pitch level
3. Relative intonation
4. Uniformity of response
5. Stability

1. Quality of tone will depend upon the type of reed used and to some extent on the individual technique of the person trying the oboe. However, some instruments inherently have a fuller, deeper, and more resonant tone than others. Only a skilled and experienced oboist can make this evaluation.

2. In general, oboes are pitched too low. Such instruments require either the use of a small reed or a tight embouchure to get up to or above A = 440. Personally, I prefer an instrument which will comfortably play at A = 440 with a reed tube length of 46-47 mm. and a total reed length of 68-70 mm. A new instrument with this pitch level may get slightly sharper with use. The use of a device like the Stroboconn is ideal for determination of pitch. Plus or minus twenty "cents" (a "cent" is 1/100th of a semitone) is a permissible deviation in pitch, since it can readily be compensated for by adjusting the dimensions of the reed.

3. The relative intonation of various registers on the oboe itself is also important. Small corrections can be made by adjusting the size of the tone hole or the height of the pad. For instance, if the G is both stuffy and flat, raising the F♯ key or enlarging the F♯ hole would probably cure the difficulty. A sharp C♯ could be lowered by lowering its pad or slightly filling the C♯ hole. These adjustments should only be made by a qualified person.

4. Occasionally an instrument will have several weak, unresponsive notes. Unless this finding can be traced to faulty adjustment or leaky pads it should be sufficient ground for rejection of the oboe.

5. Similarly, if the oboe is unstable—that is, if it sags or gurgles on some notes—it should be rejected. Defects in the dimensions of the bore will often cause low notes to be so unstable that it is almost impossible to produce a controlled *pianissimo*. If this is true of notes above the low C♯, reject the instrument.

The majority of professional players in the United States still use oboes of French manufacture, and these instruments are among the best obtainable for quality and price. I have used a Lorée for twenty years. Other recommended makes are Chauvet, Marigeaux, Rigoutat, and Cabart. Of American makers, Alfred Laubin seems outstanding. Other well-known makers are Conn, Linton, Selmer, Larilee, Platz, and Lym.

Most professional players in this country use the Conservatory system. It usually has covered holes, a low B-C♯ trill, side F, and F resonance keys. Many oboes with open holes and without extra trill keys are being used in schools because they are cheaper and easier to maintain. The lack of extra keys may be an inconvenience, but the prime considerations should be the stability of the tone quality and the relative intonation of the instrument. Every player should have as fine an oboe as can be obtained. Since good equipment is expensive and requires proper care, very young students should not be encouraged to start on the oboe. High school is early enough, and children of high-school age not only will take better care of the oboe but will also have less difficulty in covering the keys and controlling the instrument.

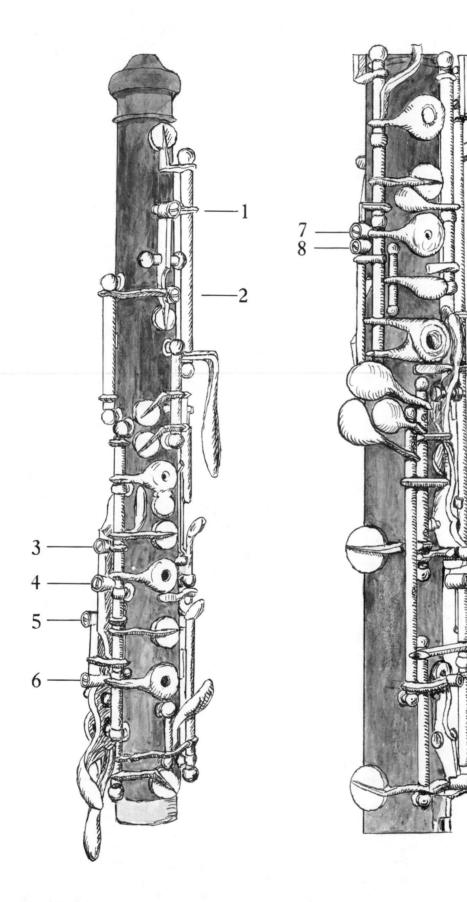

ILLUSTRATION 1

Adjusting the Mechanism

Every oboist needs a basic understanding of how to make simple mechanical adjustments. He should know what to look for and when and where to use the screw driver. Most problems arise from slight leaks under one or more pads. These leaks usually result from worn or lost adjusting corks, or possibly from a slightly bent key. Plateaux (covered-hole) oboes have numerous set screws whose purpose is solely that of regulating the height of the keys they control. Proper adjustment of these screws is essential. The accompanying diagram (Illust. 1) shows the set screws normally encountered on a good covered-hole instrument. They are numbered and discussed in order.

Set screws *1* and *2*, which regulate the height of the octave keys, are not of great importance. The small keys between the B and A keys and between the A and G keys, however, are frequent sources of trouble. Several screws are used to regulate them. Number *3* regulates the height of the C key — the small pad between the first and second fingers. If, with the second finger down, the pad stays open even very slightly when the F♯ key is closed, screw *3* should be turned slightly clockwise. If it is too tight, the A key will require excessive finger pressure to close, and screw *3* will have to be loosened by turning it counterclockwise until both pads close with equal tension. This can be checked with a sliver of cigarette paper. Slide the paper under the C key and, with the keys held down normally, pull the paper out gently. Repeat this process under the A key. If either pad seems to hold the paper too loosely or too tightly, the proper adjustment should be made.

The other screws can be adjusted as follows: Number *4* should only be tight enough for the spring action to close the C and B♭ keys equally. Number *5* regulates the height of the C♯ and B♭ pads when the first finger key of the right hand is pressed down to play C♯ or B♭. If it is too tight the pads will be held open even when the F♯ key is released.

Number *6* regulates the connection to the B♭ pad. If it is too tight, the G key will stay open, and if it is too loose the pad will open when the F♯ key is put down.

Number *7* regulates the pad between the first and second fingers of the right hand when the E key is closed. Tightness will allow the E key to stand open, whereas with looseness the pad will fail to close. Number *8* regulates the same pad

through the D key. Again, tightness will keep the finger pad (D key) open, and looseness will cause the small key to remain slightly open.

Number *9* regulates the C♯-D♯ trill. Tightening it (turning it clockwise) will close the D♯ key when the C♯ key is down. Extreme tightness will cause the C♮ pad to stay open.

Number *10* regulates the left side E♭ key. If it is too loose there will be lost action. If it is too tight, the E♭ key will be held open.

Number *11* regulates the low B♭ pad in relation to the low B pad. Tightening it lowers the B♭. However, if the B pad doesn't cover, the screw must be loosened until both pads close with equal tension. This can be checked visually and by the use of a sliver of cigarette paper.

Number *12* regulates the height of the C♯ key.

Number *13* regulates the low B-C♯ trill. Looseness will cause the C♯ pad to stay open while the B is closed. If the screw is too tight, the B pads will fail to close.

Selecting a Reed

Reeds, because of their relatively short life, will always be a problem for oboists. Since they can be made to respond and perform in a variety of ways, it is important that each player learn to make his own reeds or have a source on which he can depend. Reedmaking is discussed in detail in Part II of this book.

The best source for buying reeds is a professional player who augments his income by making reeds. In general, the imported French reeds (in contrast to the French oboes) are of poor quality.

For the beginner, the main considerations in selecting a reed should be ease of blowing, a small opening, and no flatness in pitch when blown very openly.

Soaking the Reed

Soaking the reed is an important preparation which directly affects both the reed and the embouchure. The reed can be soaked in about one-half inch of water in a small glass. When that is not convenient, good results may be obtained by filling the reed tip with saliva and returning the reed to its case or laying it on a flat surface for ten or fifteen minutes. Since food particles will clog the reed, it is not advisable to do this directly after eating.

The blades need to absorb moisture to assume their normal contours and to make them airtight on the sides. Prolonged soaking, however, especially in too deep water or in a tightly closed container, will make the reed opening too large. An over-soaked reed is unresponsive and encourages the player to bite in order to close the opening. This is dangerous because the player is usually unaware of the resulting embouchure distortion. Flexible tone control by the lip muscles becomes restricted when the reed aperture is so large that excessive jaw pressure must be used to close it.

If the aperture between blades is too small, it can usually be opened sufficiently by putting the reed in the mouth up to the binding and then alternately sucking and blowing air through it.

Producing the Tone

With an adequate reed and instrument a player should be able to produce an acceptable tone. Whether or not he does will depend largely on the effectiveness of his embouchure and the adequacy of his breath support. Let us examine these two aspects of playing.

Embouchure

Webster defines embouchure as follows: "The shaping of lips, tongue, etc., in producing a musical tone, especially on a wind instrument."

What can embouchure do for the oboe player?
1. It provides an airtight connection with the reed.
2. It provides a flexible association between the lips and the reed.
3. It places the reed in a convenient position relative to the tongue.

It is very important to assume this embouchure as simply as possible. There must not be any tensing of the jaw muscles either by jutting the chin forward or by clamping the jaws together.

Let the lower jaw drop (Illust. 2). Then place the tip of the reed about a quarter of an inch in on the red part of the lip, just about where the two lips ordinarily meet (Illust. 3). The lips and reed are then rolled up into the mouth, behind the upper teeth (Illust. 4). Do not close the jaws any more than necessary and do not pull the lips from the reed, which should rest lightly but firmly on the lower lip, supported by the lower teeth. The blades of the reed are covered gently by the lips with only about a sixteenth of an inch of the tip free inside the mouth. The feeling of this embouchure should be one of roundness, with the lips as the smaller end of a funnel which channels air into the reed efficiently and without distortion. The funnel is supported by adequate pressure against the lower teeth.

This embouchure is fairly simple to describe and assume but is not simple to maintain. By opening up the breathing apparatus and inhibiting the use of the throat and jaw muscles, we build up considerable air pressure against the lips, and this tends to force the lips out of position. The feeling of pressure is necessary and desirable in producing a fine tone, but discretion and patience must be used in cultivating adequate strength and endurance for lip control.

The lips should be placed symmetrically on the reed. Since the upper lip is shorter and less flexible, it will tend to assume a place too far down the reed, thereby exposing more of the upper blade inside the mouth. If the lower jaw normally recedes excessively, a conscious effort to push the lower jaw forward until the lips meet more evenly may be necessary. Otherwise, the upper lip will lose its correct place at the tip of the reed. The muscles that control the lips are located approximately where the red and white parts of the lip meet, and it is this portion which should be taken into the mouth to a position *behind* the upper teeth. When the "gathering" muscle is contracted and the lips puckered, the controlling surfaces or dry part of the lips will be within the mouth and in back of, rather than between, the teeth. The reed, pressing against the flesh below the lip, can and should continue to rest firmly on the lower teeth regardless of the amount of embouchure tension required on the tip of the reed inside the mouth. The embouchure should have a round shape of its own, instead of that of a tight unyielding slot or a soft spongy mass in which the reed is buried.

It is important to associate the tongue position with the embouchure formation, since its correct position is a prerequisite for adequate articulation. The tongue should lie low in the mouth with its tip resting gently against the top of the lower lip. Care should be taken to avoid setting it either under the lip or up in the way of the reed. It is imperative that the air stream have free access to the reed at all times without having to pull the tongue back in the mouth.

ILLUSTRATION 2

ILLUSTRATION 3

ILLUSTRATION 4

The correct position of the lips, reed, and tongue provides a sensitive, convenient control for both the size and shape of the aperture and the relative amount of free vibrating surface of the reed blades.

A correct oboe embouchure should result in the feeling that the air stream is comfortably directed forward and against the roof of the mouth and the upper teeth. The mouth cavity should feel big. The muscles of the face, throat, and jaw need not participate.

In outward appearance, the cane portion of the reed will be more than half way in the mouth, the lips will be turned in so that the red portion of both can scarcely be seen, and the jaws will be set fairly square.

Breath Support

Simplicity and strength of breath support are even more important than embouchure for a good oboe tone. This support is created by muscular action. Because of the great differences in strength and endurance of the several muscle groups which govern the size of the chest cavity, it is important that we consciously learn to distinguish and separate them in actual use.

Muscles are special groups of fibers which have the unique property of being able to contract when stimulated. Upon relaxing, they are resilient enough to return to their normal length to await a new stimulus. This action is like that of a solenoid with a retracting spring. Each muscle group transfers energy by shortening. Some, like the biceps, pull on a tendon which in turn pulls a bone. Others, like the diaphragm, push against other parts of the body.

Each muscle can work in only one direction, and for this reason our muscles are arranged in sets, one group pulling in one direction and its opposite group pulling in the other.

Muscles are all functional, and their development has been commensurate with their use in everyday living. Some are powerful and capable of sustained effort without fatigue. Others are comparatively weak and adapted only for control and for intermittent or unopposed action. In each case, by the process of evolution, the muscle group is well suited for the application it usually has in the body.

Playing the oboe is not a natural process, and there is little inherited instinct, feeling, or subconscious muscular action that will suit the purpose of oboe playing without proper conversion. Consequently, we must strive to use our muscles efficiently by singling out those best suited by

strength and position to do what we require. We must also learn to feel and utilize them without involving other muscles which are not needed and which may interfere with what we wish to accomplish. The ability to do away with unwanted tension is the real heart of relaxation, because it permits an unhindered channeling of our energies where we want and need them.

The regular, selective use of the proper muscles will strengthen and increase their capacity and endurance. As their efficiency improves, control increases. It should be apparent, then, that if we methodically select those muscles best suited to our purposes, and strengthen them by regular use, our technique will improve proportionately.

A vital, sustained feeling of breath and tonal support can best be derived from using the big muscles of the body. The intercostal muscles are poorly distributed for use with force, and therefore should remain passive. The player should try to cultivate instead the maximum use of abdominal support in blowing the oboe. Once we realize that the diaphragm contracts in order to take in air, it becomes obvious that the sustained force for blowing comes from the contraction of the abdominal muscles which assist the return of the diaphragm by pushing up from beneath. When we cough, or a dog barks, or a baby cries, we see this muscular action clearly. If the pressure is derived from the chest itself, we can detect it by noting that the ribs tend to collapse or go in. In learning to clarify these sensations, one may slowly huff and puff in imitation of a steam engine, trying to make the impulse come exclusively from the abdominal wall. Then one can see that the ribs, rather than actively pushing inward, react to the pressure impulses by being pushed out. The feeling of depth, power, and ease which can be cultivated in this way is very worthwhile.

Correct posture is important because the muscles involved in breath support are limited in movement and can be inhibited by unnecessary tensions. Unless the body is erect, but not stiff, and the chest comfortably filled with air before inhaling, it is difficult to cultivate the proper feeling of support. Since the action of the opposing sets of muscles is reciprocal, one set must be relaxed when the other is contracting. This is especially true when we inhale. Unless the abdominal muscles give way by relaxing, the diaphragm will not descend fully when it contracts, and the return stroke will have to be shorter. Since after the return stroke of the diaphragm is finished there can only be collapse of the chest to complete a musical phrase, the importance of this point should be apparent.

In addition to feeling "tall," we should also feel that the body is supported from below and that its parts are in alignment over a secure foundation. In a standing position the hips should be balanced over the heels, and the shoulders over the hips. The head should be comfortably up, with the neck nearly straight. This position gives maximum capacity to the chest cavity, unhindered passage for the flow of air, and free use of body muscles. When we sit, the position should be the same from the hips up.

Unfortunately, good posture is the exception rather than the rule. It is common to see people sitting or standing with their hips and head in front of their heels and shoulders. Although their equilibrium can be maintained, this is a negative position that is relatively weak and ineffectual for any muscular action. When we sit tall and at ease, our chest can be well expanded and our back will feel wider because our ribs are free of restraint.

At first this new body alignment may seem to incline the torso too far forward and the head too far backward. We must keep in mind that this only seems to be so because we have grown accustomed to a distortion. Actually, the new position looks better balanced. Be sure that the hips are not tipped forward since this arches the back and makes the abdomen too prominent. The hips should be rotated slightly backward, as in sitting down. The head and neck should not be rigid. One should feel limber and flexible.

Breathing

Breathing is so automatic that we seldom give it any thought. Simply by utilizing differences in air pressure we are able to take in and expel air. Raising the rib cage and/or lowering the diaphragm reduces the pressure in the chest so that air rushes in, while collapsing the ribs and/or relaxing the diaphragm increases the pressure so that air flows out. Normal breathing utilizes these relatively small differences in pressure.

Blowing an instrument requires extra force and control in expelling the breath. This force cannot be obtained from the diaphragm itself, because it is relaxing as we blow, and the intercostal (rib) muscles are relatively weak and ineffectual. We should therefore cultivate the use of the abdominal muscle wall to support the breath, since these strong muscles also have an excellent position of mechanical advantage.

The diaphragm is a large but relatively weak muscle which forms the floor of the chest cavity.

It is dome-shaped, arches up over the stomach, and is penetrated by the esophagus and the blood supply. When we inhale, the diaphragm flattens out and descends as it contracts; it then relaxes to its domelike position as we exhale. It is effective by itself only in non-opposed action.

The movement of the diaphragm provides enough change in air pressure to accomplish normal breathing, but mere upward relaxation is not enough to expel air quickly or powerfully. For this, another set of muscles is called into play—the abdominal muscles. Contracting them increases the intra-abdominal pressure and pushes the abdominal organs up against the diaphragm as it relaxes. This provides a strong sustained support for blowing.

Visually, it will be noted that the effort of blowing vigorously with abdominal support has the effect of expanding the chest. In consequence, the ribs are slightly pushed out. This is a simple test for correct breath support. A quick breath accent should produce the following visible effects: any point above the stomach should thrust outward slightly or remain stationary, while the abdominal wall will harden and tend to push in as it supports the upward motion of the diaphragm.

The chest may be likened to a room with the ribs as the walls, the diaphragm as the floor, and the throat as a hole in the ceiling. To get a proper sensation of using the abdominal muscles, start with the chest well expanded and take in breath by lowering the diaphragm. If the abdominal muscles are correctly relaxed, the abdomen will expand as though it were itself being filled with air. In actuality, air does not descend lower than the diaphragm. We are lowering the floor of the room and reducing the air pressure so that air is pulled into the room. By pushing the floor back up again (contracting the abdominal muscles while the diaphragm relaxes) the air pressure is increased so that air will flow out.

By restricting the use of the intercostal muscles we can increase our endurance and control in blowing. By making the weaker and ineffective muscles passive we reduce the possibility of distortion from fatigue and tension. This approach to breathing and blowing will pay handsome dividends if it is applied over a long enough period, but it is unlikely to become habitual unless it is associated with good posture. Remember that the muscles are extremely limited in the extent of their motion. The piston-like stroke of the diaphragm is controlled and strong only when there is a solid connection maintained between the abdominal muscles and the air column. When we inhale, the body should be straight and tall, with the abdominal muscles relaxed. When we blow, the abdominal muscles should contract and harden, and the chest become passive and reactive. In this way the entire muscle energy expended is directed toward inhaling or exhaling air and none of it is wasted.

The breath should be consciously taken in through the nose, but with the mouth open and relaxed. When a quick breath is required it should be taken through the mouth. Correct breathing is practically soundless and feels completely easy.

Articulation

Proper tone production, while not instinctive, can readily be learned. However, some of the necessary controls are quite unnatural and must be properly understood and applied if the tone production is not to be altered and distorted. A vivid example of this is the use of the tongue in articulation.

Articulation is the interruption of continuous sound either at the source of the breath flow or at the reed. The tongue is ideally suited for this purpose if it is used properly, because the breath support can then be continuous.

The tongue must be carefully oriented so that its tip lies in the V formed by the reed and lower lip and touches the lower blade just under the tip of the reed. While the tongue rests on the lower lip, a slight upward motion of its tip will enable it to touch the reed but still be out of the way of the flow of breath to the reed. This is important because if the tongue is given momentum by the air pressure it cannot approach the reed gently, but will invariably be pushed on violently with an unpleasant "ut" sound. Twisting the reed a few degrees counterclockwise in the oboe and inclining the instrument at a slight angle toward the left will make it easier to approach the lower lefthand corner of the reed (Illust. 5 and 6). Left-handed players may find it easier to use the opposite arrangement, that is, twisting the reed to the right and using the left side of the tongue. In any case, tonguing squarely on the opening should be avoided.

Attack

Starting a tone requires proper preparation of the lips, tongue, and breath support. The lips should be set in position to produce the desired pitch and dynamic level. The tongue should be placed as directed in the preceding section, with its tip stopping the tone by lightly touching the corner of the reed. The breath support should then be asserted before the tongue is withdrawn from the reed. Support can be assured by feeling the breath pressure in the mouth directed at the upper teeth.

The attack is made by quickly dropping the tip of the tongue to permit air to flow through the reed. The tone should continue at a steady intensity until the tongue returns to the reed (unless the lips or breath are altered). This action fits naturally with the pronunciation of a "T." Note that the tongue moves up and down instead of back and forth.

Place the hand in front of the lips and pronounce the letter "D" and then the letter "T." Observe that the "T" gives a little push to the air. The tongue moves as a whole for the "D," merely releasing whatever breath we choose to give as support, but for the "T" an additional small burst of air is contributed as the middle portion of the tongue pushes up while the tip quickly drops down out of the way. This "T" type of action gives clarity to all kinds of articulation and, being both vigorous and yet controlled, helps to overcome the inertia of the air column without the danger of overblowing. Furthermore, it is practical and desirable for all dynamic ranges. Since holding back the breath support or trying to attack gently both tend to make soft playing hazardous, it is not necessary to articulate differently for *pianissimo* notes. However, tonguing either *pp* or low register notes may also be effectively visualized as a lifting motion of the tip of the tongue, since the lips cover the blades more completely. As before, the underside of the tongue should maintain contact with the lower lip and care should be taken not to block the opening of the reed with the tongue.

Associating syllables with this motion can be of value. Each articulated note would be thought of as one syllable, not two. For this reason syllables like "tee" or "ton" are good. A succession of tongued notes would look like this: tee(t) tee(t) tee(t), or ton(t) ton(t) ton(t), etc., rather than ta-ut ta-ut ta-ut. The end of each note serves as a complete preparation for the next, without audible distortion of quality or dynamics and without alteration of the air column support. Of course, the ends of phrases or of isolated notes do not require this preparation for the next note and can be properly tapered off with the lips. Ordinarily, the last note before a breath is taken should not be stopped with the tongue.

The terms "attack" and "release" are misnomers. Since the tongue is withdrawn from the

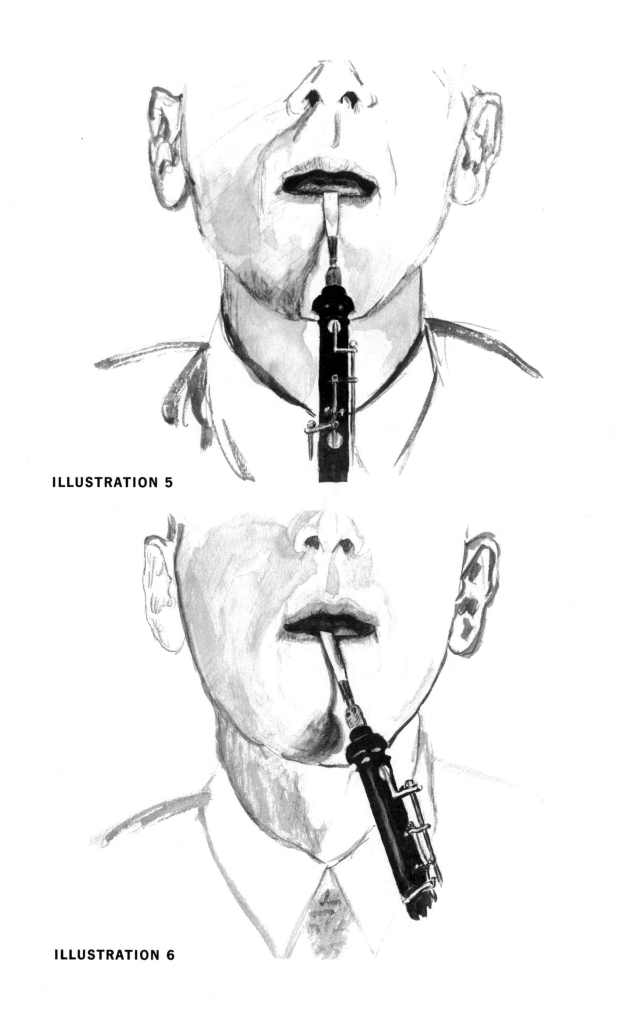

ILLUSTRATION 5

ILLUSTRATION 6

15

reed to start the tone, this action could more properly be described as a release. Similarly, stopping the tone (since we return the tongue to the reed) is really more like an attack. The prime considerations are to have the tongue in the most convenient position and to regulate its movements so that there is a minimum of distortion to the support and flow of the breath.

We are instinctively repelled by the sound of the tongue abruptly blocking the opening of the reed while the tone is fully supported. The natural reaction is to avoid this "ut" sound. The usual solution is to let up on the breath support to cover up the sound of the tongue, and to hold the tongue far back in the mouth so that it is well out of the way of the reed. This may help to avoid the worst effects, but does not completely solve the original problem; in addition, it contributes toward an uneven dynamic level and a devitalized tone.

We must learn to manage the tongue so skillfully that it cannot be heard returning to the reed. Unless breath pressure can be maintained independently of articulation, phrasing and tone quality will both be distorted because of the unintentional rise and fall of the air pressure.

If the tongue is held too far from the reed its motions cannot be subtly controlled. It will hit the reed instead of touching it gently. Its motion even causes additional air pressures which con-tribute distortions of their own.

Musically, it is natural and desirable to think of the tone as flowing at a regular rate of speed. One should realize, however, that in *staccato* and other articulated passages the flow of air is intermittent, and a smaller quantity of air passes through the reed in a given length of time. This is why less blowing effort is needed for *staccato* than for *legato* playing. However, the reservoir of breath pressure should remain unaffected by the necessary tongue action. This independence of tonal support from articulation results in a sensation very much like holding your breath instead of blowing note by note.

If holding the tongue close to the reed encourages a "tha" type of attack, it is because the tongue is not being moved away from the reed quickly enough. The correct position can be maintained and the tip of the tongue will move more quickly if a clear "T" sound is pronounced. The return of the tongue to the reed should always be gentle unless the note being played is extremely short. Fast-tongued passages in the low register can be improved by covering the reed a little more with the upper lip and a little less with the lower. This gives the tongue more room to move.

The air column should be like a big standpipe of air. Its flow through the reed is articulated like the turning of a faucet on and off.

Controlling the Tone

Intonation

Powerful disruptive forces result from the divergent tuning tendencies of various musical instruments. Each performer should know not only the deviation tendencies of his own instrument, but also those of his neighbors'. The use of an accurate, impartial device like the Stroboconn is perfect for measuring the extent of these divergences. This information, to be useful, must be properly interpreted in an unemotional and objective way which is only possible in an atmosphere of mutual respect and co-operation.

Even under ideal circumstances, temperature and humidity changes affect various instruments in different degrees, and even in opposite directions. For instance, an air column vibrates faster as the temperature rises, but a string or bar vibrates slower because it expands. Thus, during a concert, unadjusted strings would normally become flatter while the wind instruments would tend to get sharper. The string players have yet another problem in the perfect fifths between their strings, for each descending fifth from the tuning note becomes two "cents" flatter. This makes the C string six "cents" flatter than it would be in the tempered scale. It is natural, therefore, that performers will constantly adjust their strings to be in tune with the pitch they hear from the rest of the orchestra. Wind players are generally belligerent about the tuning problem and blame the rising pitch inclination on the string players. A more realistic view shows that, although it takes time, faith, and understanding to get the string players to tune down, the real reason they go up is self-defense. In general, the string sections mirror the pitch of the winds.

A related phenomenon is the compulsion to prefer the higher of two pitches. In most cases a listener would say the lower pitch was flat rather than the higher pitch sharp. Conductors are especially guilty of encouraging the "sharp" offenders, for they rarely censure them, instead often blaming the player who is striving not to give in to the cheap and easy rise in pitch. It takes understanding and courage to tackle the tuning problem in any ensemble properly, especially since one or two conscientious persons cannot solve it alone, and a few careless ones can make the situation difficult for everyone else.

More specifically, each player should know the pitch discrepancies of his own instrument and refuse to give in to them. He must resist the temptation to tune the general level of his instrument sharper in order to make other players flat to him. Ensemble playing is a democratic process, and the pitch problem can only be solved by sharing it. The low-register notes on the flute and oboe are definitely on the flat side, whereas on the clarinet they are easily blown sharp. If, for instance, the flutist plays the A=440 softly while tuning, almost inevitably all the second and third octave notes will tend to be sharp. The B on the B♭ clarinet is usually a flat note. If it is brought up to pitch by shortening the barrel, the instrument as a whole will be too sharp — especially the throat notes and the notes above the staff. Brass players have similar problems. There are certain notes that will always be on the low side and others on the high side. Instead of tuning to avoid being flat we must consistently strive to improve our control and flexibility so we can adhere to correct pitch level at all times. Good intonation is one of the most necessary and satisfying conditions for making and listening to music, yet it is the most frequently abused because of the failure of some players to realize that each individual must accept his share of the responsibility for its maintenance. An orchestra of 100 players is as dependent on this attitude of individual responsibility as a string quartet, but it is rare to find a large group where this principle is properly recognized. The decision to play at 440 cycles per second for A is arbitrary and completely without virtue in itself. It is only useful if everyone adheres to it as the common meeting place. The mistaken idea that being sharp will provide brilliance to the tone is a cheap way of taking advantage of the other players, because sharpness is a comparative condition and can only exist when someone else is flat. The same divergences will exist at A=445, A=450, or any other value. Any reasoning person knows that the best sonority comes from being in tune, not in being sharp or

flat. If the tuning note is obtained from a reliable, impersonal source, preferably electronic, there is much more likelihood that it will be accepted without "interpretation." When a performer gives the A, some people tune sharp in anticipation that he is flat or unreliable. In general, fear of being flat, lack of faith in other players, and plain carelessness are the principal factors which undermine pitch stability.

We should tune carefully, even when we are playing alone, since we base our whole feeling for tone production upon the pitch level that we associate with individual notes and registers. If we come to a general rehearsal or a performance and have to change our tuning level very much, our tonal feeling can be so disrupted that we are reluctant to change tuning enough.

There is a variety of opinion about the exact relationship for notes in a scale. Some musicians favor the Pythagorean tuning, some the "just" intonation, and others the "tempered" scale. The choice depends largely upon whether one is thinking harmonically or melodically. We probably use them all at different times and in different passages, but only the "just" intonation will tune vertically through chords. In any case, the differences in these systems of tuning are less than the errors that usually offend our ears because of carelessness. Learning to play in tune is a complicated process, requiring sensitivity, control, and understanding. A desire to cooperate is essential.

Finger Technique

Another source of trouble is the way the instrument is fingered. The oboe is awkward to hold comfortably because of the spacing of the keys, so time spent in cultivating a relaxed and efficient hand position is worthwhile. Not only is finger technique involved, but tone and tone control as well, since any change in the balance of the instrument is immediately transmitted to the embouchure. A tight, biting type of embouchure usually accompanies a heavy-handed finger action in order to hold the oboe more securely; a sensitive and open embouchure requires only balanced and gentle finger control.

Hand and Finger Position

Attainment of maximum control with minimum effort requires good posture and correct breathing, so that any unnecessary tensions in the body are released.

The hand position, with the fingers poised over the keys, should be as comfortable as possible. The fingers should be slightly curved and

ILLUSTRATION 7

18

without excess tension, touching the keys with the soft pads of their tips. The right hand is difficult to relax because of the necessity of supporting the oboe on the thumb. This support is easiest at a point just back of the thumbnail. The right arm and fingers are normally parallel to, or point slightly toward, the floor.

The left hand will vary in position according to the individual. Sometimes it helps to relax and curve the fingers if the palm of the left hand is held in very close to the wood of the oboe. The side octave key then comes just under the knuckle of the forefinger, and the thumb extends beyond the lower octave key, which is operated by the ball of the thumb instead of the tip. In this way the fingers can comfortably reach apart for the stretch and can come down on the instrument from above at an angle (Illust. 7). A good way to anchor the hand in a position of readiness is to keep the little finger poised over and gently touching the E♭ key.

There may be considerable variation in the appearance of the hand positions, but the playing requirements are more specific. The fingers must feel free to move, and their motion must not alter the pressure of the instrument on the lower lip. When playing with an open embouchure, the balance of the instrument should be controlled by feeling that there are three constant points of support: the right thumb, the left forefinger, and the lower jaw. These supports can and should be constantly maintained.

Finger pressure on the keys should be light. Need for more than a light pressure indicates a mechanical defect in the oboe — probably a poor

key adjustment or an ill-fitted pad. True *legato* playing is not possible unless a feeling of gentle pressure prevails, so that one can noiselessly glide from one note to another.

Co-ordination of Fingers

Accurate intervals require perfect co-ordination of the fingers. This is facilitated by keeping the fingers near and over the keys, and especially by moving them uniform distances. If two fingers are to move together, the problem of getting them to their destinations at the same time is simplified if they start at the same instant and move at the same rate of speed. A controlled distance of half an inch or less seems practical for most players.

The oboe has several finger combinations which involve lifting one key while another is coming down. At first this might appear to be a simple seesaw action, but further examination shows a more complicated effect. Whereas the lifting of a pad produces an immediate effect because the change of notes is made as soon as the finger starts to move, the lowering of a pad has a delayed effect because the change does not come until the pad closes the hole at the end of the finger movement.

Analysis shows that this natural inequality in length of notes tends to make *ascending* intervals speak faster than *descending* ones. This applies regardless of whether key action lifts a pad or the finger itself uncovers the hole. Practicing measured trills and tremolos permits a fairly accurate comparison of the duration of the two notes. Triplet motion is especially revealing, since two notes are stressed alternately.

EXAMPLE 1

This passage from the Bach *Toccata and Fugue in D Minor* dramatizes the typical distortion just described. These triplets will be difficult to play without the second note of each triplet predominating, because the upper note of each triplet tends to sound too soon.

Despite admonitions to be relaxed, to use gentle finger pressure, and to strive for a feeling of smoothness, it is still important to move

with precision and accuracy. This skill will invariably be facilitated if each fingering is carefully calculated before it is tried. Bad habits arise from blundering and fumbling for a note without visualizing the fingering. This principle applies to players of all levels of experience.

Fluent, expressive technique results from moving the fingers in a calm, precise manner. A beginner should be urged to play more than one note to a breath so that a feeling of continuous support is developed.

Rhythmic Fingering

It is essential to associate the fingering of a passage habitually with the correct rhythm. This may seem too obvious to need mention, but many rhythmic distortions stem from carelessness in this matter. There is an almost irresistible urge to execute fingerings in advance—to move ahead to the next note as soon as the previous one has stopped. Unless trained otherwise, a player will usually feel compelled to finger a *staccato* note before tonguing it. The rationalization that this is a preparation for the next note proves, on analysis, to be incorrect. Any passage which can be

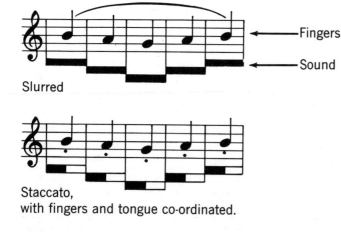

Slurred

Staccato,
with fingers and tongue co-ordinated.

Staccato, with finger anticipation
but with sound unaffected.

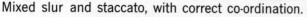

Mixed slur and staccato, with audible error
in co-ordination by anticipation of fingering.

Mixed slur and staccato, with correct co-ordination.

EXAMPLE 2

felt and fingered *legato* can and should be felt and fingered the same way when articulated. In a slow *staccato* this anticipation is least obvious, but when the tempo is speeded up, and slurs are interjected, the error is exposed. If we draw two parallel lines to represent fingering and tonguing, the time intervals on each should exactly coincide for clarity and correct rhythm. When the fingers are moved too soon, clarity and rhythm are upset.

The first of the examples shown is not a problem because the tongue is not involved in the rhythmic feeling. The second example shows *staccato* notes with the silent portion on the ends of the notes, as in correct co-ordination. In the third example an error in co-ordination is shown, which the listener can see but not hear. The rests, or silences, are at the beginning of the notes. The fourth example exposes an audible error, because the late attack is revealed when the second note of the slur sounds too soon. The irony of this error is that, instead of being analyzed properly, it is usually altered by holding the first note longer. This adds one error on top of another and inhibits the cultivation of truly rhythmic co-ordination. The fifth example shows the correct co-ordination in mixed slurs.

The key mechanism makes some assorted clicks when we raise and lower the keys. It should be noted that the click of a pad or finger *covering* a hole can and should coincide with the tongue action. However, the click made in *lifting* a finger or *raising* a key should come after the tone instead of with or before it. Therefore, when practicing a passage without blowing, it is best to move the fingers gently to minimize the sounds of the mechanism.

Finger and tongue co-ordination is not a natural result of habitual playing. Rather, it must become a consciously cultivated habit. When the fingering and tonguing are both rhythmically conceived they can and will always coincide.

The uncovering of the half-hole may be accomplished by sliding the forefinger or by rolling it slightly. Both methods are successful, but sliding has at least two advantages. It obliges the performer to play with light finger pressure, and it is less likely to distort the left-hand position. At first it may seem more difficult to learn, but this is soon overcome.

The octave-key mechanism automatically allows only one octave key to be open at a time, even when both keys are pressed together. However, it is good technique to learn to use the

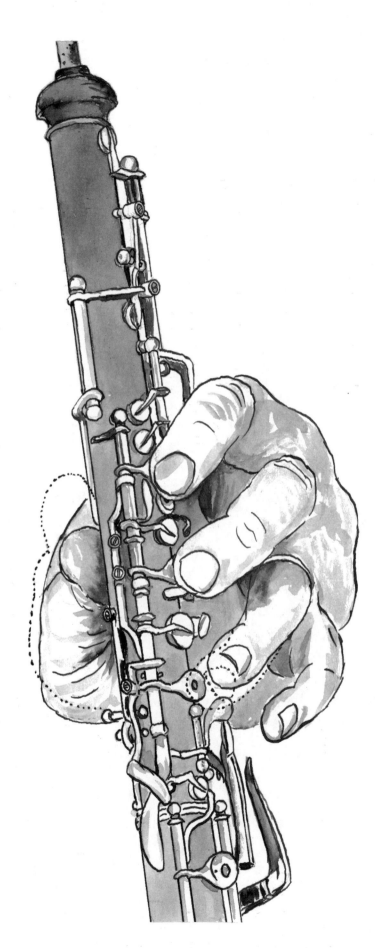

ILLUSTRATION 8

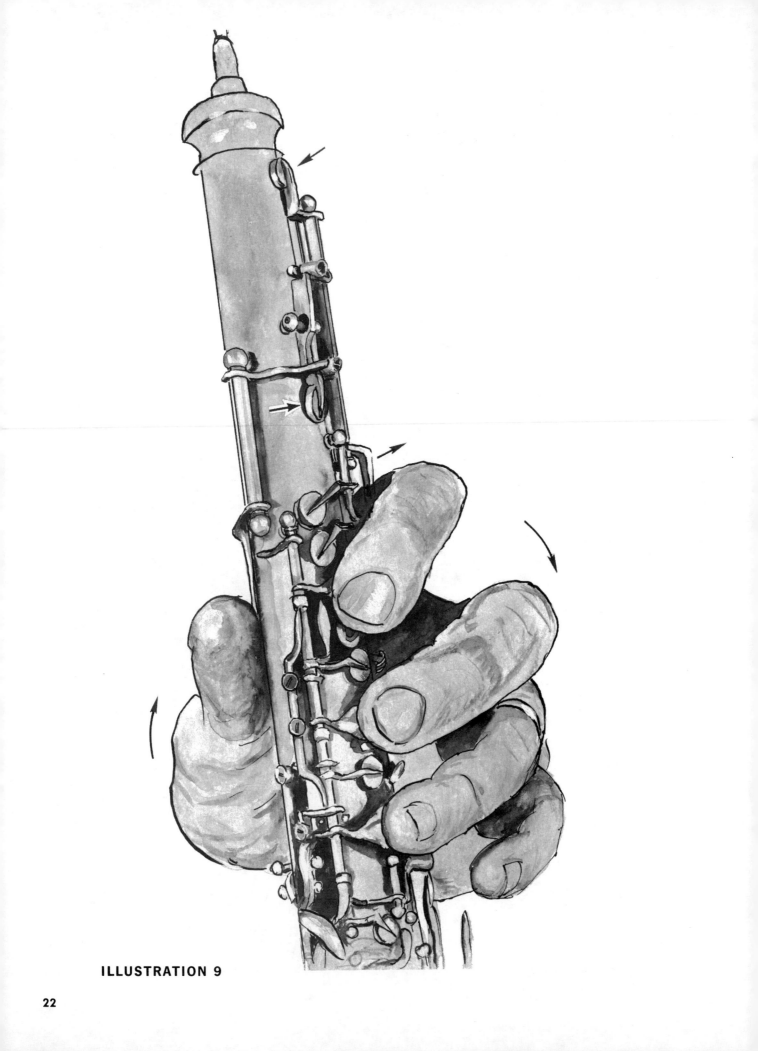

ILLUSTRATION 9

ILLUSTRATION 10

keys singly, because the motion of releasing knuckle and thumb keys together is more likely to break a *legato* line than is a motion involving only the knuckle key. If properly cultivated, the left hand will automatically make the necessary adjustment with a slight rotation of the wrist. Illust. 8, 9, and 10 show how a slight rotation of the hand can control both octave keys and the G key at the same time. In Illustration 9 the thumb octave pad is opened and the G key is closed. A smooth interval from G to A can easily be accomplished by rotating the hand so that the thumb slides off its octave key as the G key is released and the side octave key is pressed down (Illust. 10).

Dynamics

Another basic control which needs to be established and rehearsed is the ability to play with a wide dynamic range. The natural tendency is to reduce the breath support when playing softly and to blow more vigorously when playing loudly. However, important additional control can be gained by using the lips. This means of control reduces distortion in loud passages and imparts vitality to the soft ranges of tone.

Strong abdominal support, which is normal to correct blowing, produces a strong tone. Dynamic control, therefore, is primarily a process of reducing the volume of sound to the desired level either by imposing more resistance to vibration on the reed or by weakening the support. To maintain tonal intensity we must cultivate maximum control with the embouchure instead of varying the breath support. Normally, the reed should rest on the lower lip, with about one-fourth inch on the red portion of the lip. Both lips are gathered evenly about the reed, turning inward and upward and converging toward the reed tip. The jaws must be separated enough to give the lips freedom to move. As this position is exaggerated, the tone becomes softer because the lips, as they are pursed and thickened, dampen the vibration of the reed and increase its resistance. The volume of the tone is thus reduced without weakening its support and its quality. Relaxing and opening up the embouchure permits full and free vibration of the reed.

It would be incorrect to state that we should blow as vigorously for soft playing as for loud, but it is true that the sensation of support is as great or even greater in soft playing because there is less air flow. This is an effective control, but it has some potential dangers. One is the possibility of pitch distortion. The surrounding

of the reed by the lips tends to pinch the aperture, which makes the pitch sharper. To prevent going sharp we must avoid excessive pressure of the lips and distribute the dampening as evenly as possible. It is important that this control be exercised especially at the very tip of the reed. The more reed that is free inside the mouth, the more difficult the dynamic control becomes and the greater the resulting pitch distortion, because the lips are in contact with a less flexible and less vibrant part of the reed. This position also invites excess use of the jaw muscles.

Another danger arises from fatigue of the lip muscles, with the consequent substitution of throat or jaw muscles for control. Even though we may be convinced of the desirability of sustained and continuous abdominal support for a good tone, we need to maintain constant vigilance to be sure that this properly supported air column gets to the reed undistorted. Since the breath support is more powerful and quicker to develop than the embouchure, we must take care not to overwork the lips at first.

Blowing properly, we should feel air pressing against the upper teeth and roof of the mouth as though it could go directly out through the nose. The lips are apt to be pushed outward unless they are caught improperly by the teeth when their own strength gives out.

This sensation of air pressure in the mouth must continue unabated during a *diminuendo*. Frequent, brief sessions of practice are best at first, because the lips rapidly become fatigued. In fact, if beginning practice does *not* cause rapid tiring, we should be suspicious that the pressure support is being relaxed too much, that the throat is being constricted, or that the jaw muscles are being used instead of the lips.

To recapitulate, *diminuendo* is a progressively controlled *forte* accomplished by increasing the reed resistance. This is done by puckering and concentrating the lips into a small, round, thick circle of flesh on the tip of the reed. This covers and dampens the vibrations of the blades and reduces volume. It can be done without affecting articulation and without distorting the quality, pitch, or vitality of the tone.

Pitch

Playing in tune is one of the most important elements of oboe technique. It requires sensitivity and control plus reliable and properly tuned equipment. Adjusting the pitch of the oboe itself should be left to an expert. The player, however, must select and adjust reeds that will be in tune. A wide or long reed tends to be flat, while a narrow or short reed is sharper. Shortening the tubes from 48 to 43 mm. may be necessary for a very low pitched oboe.

The performer can exert a measure of pitch control by varying the size of the reed aperture. The method is similar to that used for dynamic control, with one important difference. While the maximum *dynamic* effects are obtained at the tip of the reed, the best *pitch control* is derived farther down toward the winding. The maximum reed aperture, when the embouchure is most relaxed, gives the lowest pitch. Pinching the reed opening, thus making it smaller, results in a higher pitch.

The problem is to regulate the pitch control with a minimum of distortion to the other controls. This can be done by pushing the reed farther into the mouth to play sharper and by pulling it back out to lower the pitch. The reed should not be permitted to slip on the lips. Instead, the embouchure should be sufficiently open to permit the lips to turn in and up along with the reed. The support of the reed on the lower teeth, at a point just below the red part of the lower lip, can also be varied to regulate the opening of the reed. In this way, dynamic and quality controls are still fully effective and it is comparatively easy to get back to the original pitch level by pulling the reed farther out of the mouth.

Perhaps even more important is the adjustment of the oral cavity for full resonance, since this affects tone quality as well as pitch. The use of "oo" or "aa" fills out the low register, while the higher notes gradually approach "ee." When the proper vowel is used, each tone will have maximum resonance and its best pitch. In general, the most open vowel produces the best results and should be consciously employed, especially when warming up. Some change may be necessary to "center" or focus the tone, but it should be kept to a minimum. A tone must sound in tune with itself before it can be properly tuned to an outside source, so we must first strive for a balanced tone quality and then make necessary pitch corrections.

The extent of pitch adjustment is limited. Thus, it is imperative that all other pitch factors be stabilized as much as possible. When we practice, we should base our concept of tone on the same pitch standard we expect in performance. We need to guard constantly against being a victim of a vicious cycle which almost inevitably results if the instrument is flat. The resulting

strain of sharping the pitch is fatiguing to the point that the reed tends to slide in on the lips. Since the lips have lost contact with the tip of the reed they have less dampening effect on the blades. This produces a shrill and strident tone and gives a smaller dynamic range. Unless this is properly understood we may make the mistake of compensating for the quality change by using a darker-sounding reed instead of properly using a lighter one and returning to playing on the very tip of the reed. This is another example in which an instinctive correction proves to be incorrect. For best results:

1. Play on the tip of the reed.
2. Use an open, round embouchure.
3. Use as open a vowel as possible — "oo" or "aa."
4. Tune the reed and oboe for maximum good tone and dynamic range.
5. Use more reed inside the lips to play sharper. Use a shallow vowel ("ee") only for temporary corrections.
6. Listen, project, and listen!

Vibrato

In music, vibrato is a word closely related to quality, expressiveness and intensity. Physically, it denotes an observable phenomenon affecting the tone itself. This may be described as regular, recurring cycles of intensity or of pitch variation (or both) in the tone. Generally speaking, vibrato on stringed instruments or in the voice consists of almost equal parts of pitch and intensity variations. To qualify as a vibrato, the pulsing must be sufficiently regular and unobtrusive as to enhance, rather than distort, the tone. It must be produced in a fluent, flexible way which does not interfere with tone production or control.

Vibrato is a personal and expressive phase of our technique, but it can be examined objectively. It can be felt as an integral part of the tone, not as an added ingredient, if the muscles involved are basic in the breath support. The abdominal and diaphragm muscles work in opposition and, when under proper tension, contract alternately to cause a recurring intensity wave in the tone.

We can consciously produce this muscular action at slow speeds by imitating the sound of a steam engine. Although this procedure fits our requirements in the sense that it involves the strong and basic blowing muscles, the vibrato will not become fluent and unobtrusive until the muscles are set at the right tension to make action and reaction self-perpetuating and continuous. This is important because as long as we consciously make each pulse, the vibrato will feel and sound artificial.

The individual intensity impulses tend to fuse together into a warmly vibrant sound as we approach the speed of five cycles per second. The maximum speed obtainable is about seven cycles per second, which is the physiologic limit of response. Consequently, the expressive range of the vibrato is between five and seven cycles per second. When learning to make these pulsations, we should concentrate on smoothness, symmetry, and ease of production rather than on speed. Unfortunately, the urge to use the vibrato for a better sound results in an emphasis on speed. This is another situation in which expediency often inhibits the possibility of developing a basically correct technique.

At first, the inexperienced player tends to exaggerate the use of the abdominal muscles and finds speed difficult to achieve. However, as the pulsating sensation becomes familiar, and the tension is confined to only the necessary muscles, the desirable range of five to seven pulses per second becomes more readily attainable.

The pulsing breath support in this type of vibrato is reflected in the tonal intensity, which fluctuates in direct proportion to the amount of air pressure change. It will be observed that a wide variation in intensity makes a more obvious, or wider, vibrato, while a small variation is scarcely noticeable. The ability to vary the width and speed of the vibrato consciously, independent of dynamics, will greatly enhance its expressiveness.

Vibrato is continuously produced (except for special effects) when it is properly conceived as part of the tone. Progressions of notes in a passage, rhythms, pitches, and speeds should all be independent of the vibrato, as it should be independent of them. Vibrato is not only used for long notes; it is produced as part of the basic tone quality to enhance both fast and slow notes. Key points to remember about vibrato are:

1. It should be part of the tone.
2. It should be unobtrusive.
3. It should be smooth.
4. It should be independent of dynamics.
5. It should be independent of pitch.
6. It should be independent of notes (speed, rhythm, etc.).

Another consideration worth mentioning is that the process of thinking about and analyzing vibrato has the effect of making the tone seem less desirable. In other words, it spoils our perspective on tone by making us so conscious of its parts that we lose the feeling for the whole sound. However, this is only a temporary condition. The beneficial results are far-reaching and permanent, whereas the apparently harmful results are only transient.

Vibrato reflects a normal human craving for warmth and vitality in tone production. It is readily imitated, which explains why some players have an excellent vibrato without particular effort or awareness. Others are handicapped with tonal distortions which they call vibrato, and which were just as innocently acquired. Habits already established are particularly difficult to change, so it is advisable to keep close watch on young players and help them to form a proper conception of this phase of their technique.

Vibrato can also be produced by the lips, the tongue, the hands, and the throat. Of these, the throat vibrato is the most commonly used. Its chief disadvantages are the restriction of the flow of breath and the loss of the smooth, symmetrical tone characteristic of the diaphragm vibrato. This is a result of air pressure being built up by the constriction of the throat and then being released spasmodically. Throat vibrato tends to sound shallow and impetuous and seems to be added to the tone instead of being a part of it.

An observant student, upon having this explained to him, remarked that perhaps one could profitably visualize the vibrato as a pendulum-like motion. Trying to start a pendulum from the top (the throat) is awkward and inefficient, but when the force is applied at the bottom (the diaphragm), the pendulum cycle is readily induced. In both cases the top of the pendulum is moving, but in the first case it is active motion and in the second, passive. The throat does participate in vibrato, but not actively. It merely responds to and transmits the impulses from below. Throat vibrato *subtracts* energy from the tone while diaphragm vibrato *adds* vitality.

Problems of Phrasing

Considered alone, correct mechanical execution is neither musical nor unmusical. Learning to manipulate the oboe is only a means to the end, that is, the playing of music. Even a serious technical deficiency is more pardonable than musicianship which is insensitive or careless.

Many exacting demands are made upon us as players. Musical notation is quite precise with regard to speed, rhythm, dynamics, articulation and breathing. But in the very important field of phrasing, the instructions are vague. Since even excellent oboists have difficulty in fulfilling all the exacting details of a composition, and since, measured by absolutes, most of us would be found wanting in perfection, we have ample motive to continue to increase our technical resources of control, speed, flexibility, and endurance. We must also continually search for a more complete, vivid, and expressive concept of how the music should sound. It is the phrasing, so vaguely indicated but so all-important, which subtly and expressively displays our understanding of what we play. A musical phrase is as full of inflections and stresses as a phrase in poetry, yet in both cases the interpretive clues are not apparent on the printed page.

Spontaneity and poise are essential to good phrasing because they give the necessary perspective to see where the music is going. The notes that are being played must constantly be related in the player's mind to the notes that are yet to come. Only in this way can the marks of expression, both written and implied, be evaluated. For instance, ♪♪♪♪ to a beat cannot be accurately timed unless the following beat, even if it is silent, is also vividly felt. For this reason it is helpful to group such patterns mentally in other ways than the obvious 1 2 3 4   1 2 3 4.

If one thinks ___ 2 3 4   1 , or
4 1 2 3 4   1 2 3 4 or 1 2 3 4 1 2 3 4,
it often is more meaningful and may help counter any error of standardization.

Dynamic marks require similar perspective. In *diminuendo* the ▭ has to be timed and gauged by the shape of the phrase. In fact, the right amount of expressive inflection can best be decided only as one approaches the points of melodic and rhythmic stress or repose in the music. This is why we need to concentrate on intervals, progressions, and groups of notes rather than on individual notes. Isolated notes may be correctly played, but to be played musically they must be expressively related to each other. This can only be done by constant visual and mental probing ahead so as to select the appropriate amount of inflection. Since we are not machines, this will vary slightly every time a phrase is played.

Mechanics of Notation

The mechanics of musical notation require symbols arranged in an orderly fashion on the page. These methods have been dictated by tradition and convenience. The way the notes, lines, figures, etc., appear usually has little in common with the composer's inspiration, even though the values designated may be accurate. The eye unconsciously assigns some width to bar lines, extra weight to long notes, grouping to notes of a common flag (series of eighths, sixteenths, etc.), anticipation to accents, and many other unmusical cliches. These compulsions are natural and almost universal, but because they interfere with the listener's comprehension of the musical content as a whole, they are wrong.

We must consciously divorce our concept of the music from its appearance and concentrate instead on how it should sound. Before the music can be properly phrased, the mathematical symmetry of the note progressions and the melodic and harmonic cadences must be fully comprehended. Skillful management can give balance to an expressive phrase without violating the written instructions. Indeed, this interpretation or reading between lines is necessary to recreate the composer's ideas.

String players use the term "phrasing" to indicate a series of notes executed with one bow stroke, but here it refers to any grouping of notes by inflection rather than merely by their rhythms or by the way they are to be articulated. Inflection may entail variations in dynamic level or in amplitude and frequency of the vibrato, slight *tenutos,* and even small distortions of time values. Used singly or in combination, these effects imply progression and are calculated to tie together and stress certain notes, making them part of a moving group. Inflections usually involve groups of two or three notes which may be part of a longer phrase.

Technical Hazards

The inflections of good phrasing are so subtle that they require an undistorted technique to be effective. This is especially apparent when articulation is inadequate. When breath support must be interrupted in order to start or to stop the notes, the phrase line will invariably be distorted. Broad note grouping, so much a part of good phrasing, becomes impossible when the dynamic intensity of individual notes tends to rise and fall simply because they are articulated. Many phrases coincide with the tonguing, but they should remain technically independent of it. Do not limit the phrasing by the mechanics of articulation.

Another series of unmusical inflections is derived from heavy-handed fingering. Often in the process of cultivating accurate finger technique, excessive energy is used in moving the fingers. This makes the balance of the instrument vary according to the number of fingers down, with resultant unmusical nuances. The finger pressure should be kept light and graceful, because, unless we operate the keys without disturbing the balance of the instrument, the reed will move around on the lips and cause pitch and dynamic variations which are not intended. This is especially noticeable when a correct and open embouchure is used, because the jaws, not being clamped on the reed, cannot hold it still.

Lack of proper co-ordination between fingers and tongue, especially habitual anticipation with the fingers, gives an unintended inflection to the notes. This distortion is most unpleasant in passages with both slurred and tongued notes, because the first tone in each slurred group is foreshortened. Comparison between this tone and the next, which will be the correct length, causes the rhythmic feeling to lose conviction (see Finger Technique, p. 17).

Careless and haphazard breathing often breaks the line of an extended passage. Breathing should be planned in advance to enhance the interest of a phrase rather than to distort it. Stopping for breath in the midst of a musical phrase offends the listener as much as does stopping in the middle of a word.

Embellishments must be conceived and executed within the phrasing. Turns, mordents, and trills are merely ornaments and should not interrupt the feeling of a phrase or change its inflection.

It should be realized that many factors operate to break a musical line. Furthermore, our desire to perfect each detail of a passage also favors a note-by-note conception. These tendencies must be minimized by learning to see and hear the broad lines of the music. Fine music, properly understood, makes sense. When played well, it lives by progressing from one idea to the next with conviction and imagination. Phrasing is the means by which we co-ordinate and project our feelings of motion, life, and intensity in music. It is essential that the mechanics of playing our instrument in no way obstruct this projection and that our basic technique be so fluent as to permit an unhindered transfer from our minds to the actuality of sound.

Accents

Designation of accents varies so much that there is confusion on how to interpret and execute them. Actually $>$, *fp*, *sfz*, and *fzp* can all be played as $f \supset p$. That is, the first part of the note is abnormally loud and the rest of it falls quickly back to the dynamic level of the passage as a whole. It must be recognized that accented notes are not just loud notes or notes in *diminuendo,* but that their effectiveness depends upon the suddenness of the drop in level and upon the relative duration and contrast of the two levels.

Tonal support and embouchure control are the keys to the correct production of accents. The loud beginning of the note is made by a sudden abdominal contraction while the embouchure is simultaneously opened slightly to permit the surge of air to have full effect. The abrupt volume decrease is accomplished by a quick tightening of the embouchure. Normal articulation, pronouncing a clear "T" consonant, is all that is required. Accents are almost entirely made by breath support. Violent tongue action has little effect, as a bit of experimenting will show. Play any note, tonguing it as vigorously as possible, then make a *diminuendo* with the lips while continuing to tongue. The attack gets softer along with the dynamic level.

Accents are special effects which are used to give rhythmic or melodic stress to isolated notes in a passage. We must take care not to destroy the phrase line or the general dynamic level either by a wrong effect or by overexaggeration of the right one. In a slow passage, a note with an accent may, as a phrase member, also need a *crescendo* for which there will be no time unless the accent is quickly and properly effected. It must not be forgotten, however, that accents of all kinds do have length. The *forte* part is not instantaneous and may, on longer notes, have a value equal to a quarter or a half of the note. Most accents written for the oboe are melodic rather than percussive, yet the temptation is to play them all percussively. Similarly, a temptation to anticipate must also be inhibited.

Problems of Practice

Musicians are often so engrossed in the details of their work that they fail to perceive the strong natural forces which oppose their efforts to improve. One of these is the ready acceptance of familiar acts as the natural or right way to do a thing. This is so deep-seated that it usually requires outside observation to point out the inconsistencies. For this reason, we can profit from listening to records of our playing and from watching movies of our efforts. Use of a mirror is also helpful. Many times we unknowingly violate principles to which we readily subscribe intellectually, because we lack the necessary perspective. We never really get to know how we sound to others, and consequently we must continually condition our feeling of what is right until it is more nearly representative of an effect which is acceptable to ourselves and to our auditors.

Practicing is a dangerous business! Judgment and common sense must be used at all times to regulate our daily practicing efforts so that a better mastery of the instrument is apparent. Several conditions should prevail.

1. We should have a detailed and thorough understanding of the physical principles of playing.
2. We should isolate the required controls and concentrate on them separately while rejecting unwanted habits.
3. We should be objective instead of emotional about rehearsing, streamlining, and conditioning these controls.
4. We should take the long view in cultivating our technique and should pursue accurate, flexible goals that will become increasingly effective.
5. We should devote regular, adequate time to practicing.

Unless we have unusual perspective and/or good instruction, we are bound to develop bad habits which are not apparent to us, and everyday practicing will strengthen and perpetuate the very errors we need to eliminate.

In performance an expedient method may be justifiable. But our only hope of outgrowing expediencies is to practice always as correctly as possible. Consequently, privacy is needed for practice, since it is tempting to "perform" when we know someone is listening. When practicing, we should deliberately probe and expose weaknesses regardless of any embarrassment involved. A typical practice session could be as follows:

1. A mental review of the elements of good posture.
2. Some exaggerated breathing, thinking about the depth, strength, and ease required to create the necessary air pressure for blowing.
3. Careful attention to the reed to assure the proper aperture, response, etc., before playing. This is important. If the opening is too large we will have to bite to produce an adequate tone. If the reed leaks air, the resistance will be excessive and the response unreliable. Of course, if the opening is not large enough we will not get the proper sensation of air flowing through the reed.
4. Play some long tones, preferably around low D or E♭, merely sustaining them while trying to feel the tone with maximum resonance and strength. There must be no distortion or agitation or feeling of "holding up" the tone, and the resulting pitch and quality should be good and firm.
5. Play slow, measured trills. This is a revealing and useful practice device. It permits observation of intervals, and the transition from one note to another is much more difficult than sustaining one note. Even when concentrating on tone production, certain other defects that tend to creep in can be distinguished. One defect is the unequal time response between lifting and closing a pad. Another is in the balance or equilibrium of the instrument—

the finger motion must not move the instrument and reed and thus affect the tone production. If too much reed is exposed inside the mouth, the tone quality is more apparent because the intervals sound abrupt.

(meter and pitches may be varied
at the performer's discretion)

EXAMPLE 3

This is the foundation upon which playing is based. It should be simple, vivid, and pleasurable so that it can be readily experienced both as a "sound" and as a "feeling." The amount of time devoted to this part of practicing will depend upon how successfully the desired end is accomplished. At first it may consume the entire practice period. Later, as results come more readily, less time will be required.

During this warm-up period the embouchure should be checked to make certain that the lips are in the optimum position, that is, gently encircling the tip of the reed. Only in this way can the dynamics be controlled without having to alter the way we blow. The tongue position should also be checked. Unless the tip of the tongue is practically touching the lower corner of the reed, the articulation will be too awkward to be accomplished with the tongue alone. At the same time the angle of the reed and instrument can be checked to assure the best position for the lips to cover the blades as symmetrically as possible. If the oboe is held up too nearly horizontal, the upper lip tends to move down the reed and to expose more of the tip of the upper blade. This makes the tone quality less controlled and the pitch somewhat sharper.

6. When the tone production has been established in a satisfactory manner, the various controls should be rehearsed. Practicing *diminuendos* is a good example. Start the tone with full volume and gradually increase the encircling and covering of the reed blades by the lips, causing

the volume to diminish. Meanwhile keep constant the support against the flesh below the lower lip. It is important that this is practiced regularly so that reliable dynamic control is achieved without reducing the breath support of the tone or undermining the resonance and feeling of depth.

7. After considerable success with *diminuendos*, we should practice *ff* $>$ *pp* $<$ *ff*.
8. Then *pp* $<$ *ff* $>$ *pp*.
9. Next, turn to articulation, concentrating on the simplicity of the tongue motion used to stop and start the tone. Sustain a note long enough to feel its depth and resonance and then stop it with the tongue. If it stops unexpectedly or too abruptly, the tongue position is not advantageous and must be calculated with more care. Be sure that the tone production continues unchanged so that the only variable is the manner in which the tongue is manipulated. The clarity of the attack depends upon the speed and neatness of removing the tongue from the reed. Satisfactory release of the tone depends upon the gentleness with which the tongue returns to the reed. The co-ordination of the position of the tongue, reed, and lips is critical and needs continual checking. We must be sure that the throat does not constrict and that the tone continues to be produced in the same manner as for sustained notes.

EXAMPLE 4

10. When a satisfactory feeling for the articulation has been established, we should have sufficient perspective to combine dynamic controls and articulation. An excellent exercise is *ff* $=$ *pp* with separated tones, each one softer than the one before. Care should be taken to keep constant support and to make the separation only with the tongue. This exercise can be elaborated to form a scale as follows:

EXAMPLE 5

The apparent simplicity of this exercise will be deceiving to those who have never tried it. Excellent control is needed to make seven gradations of dynamics on each step of the chromatic scale, while at the same time controlling the dynamics with the lips and the articulation with the tongue. Breath may be taken not oftener than every two measures, and a vigorous, deep quality of tone must always be present. Beginners should start with four or five shades of intensity. Care should be taken to make the slur to the next scale step as smooth and *legato* as possible.

Vibrato may be added at any point in the above sequence. However, its use *must not distort tone production.* Since vibrato itself is an element of tone, it in turn should not be disturbed by articulation or by variations in register or dynamics. Sometimes just thinking about vibrato is enough to induce its production. On the other hand, many talented and otherwise accomplished players have difficulty with it. In any case, proper practice will improve its effectiveness.

After a deep, solid, straight tone can be produced (Step 4), the tone can be made to pulsate by alternately increasing and decreasing air pressure. Exaggerated contraction and relaxation of the abdominal muscle is an effective way to begin, even though it is ponderous and clumsy at first. Fluent and easy production comes naturally only when the diaphragm and possibly the intercostal muscles begin to participate too. This cannot be readily induced because we do lack a direct sensation of diaphragm control. The pulse from the contraction of the abdominal muscles is the positive phase, and the contraction of the diaphragm muscle is the negative phase of the recurring cycle of air pressure changes. When this reciprocal action can be easily induced as a continuous sensation, a true and useful vibrato will appear.

Step 5, if practiced with vibrato, will expose any attempt to start and stop the vibrato with each note. A feeling of continuity becomes easier when the pulse speed rate reaches five per second. Steps 6, 7, and 8, practiced with vibrato, help to assure independence of vibrato from dynamic control. Steps 9 and 10 should be practiced to insure that the vibrato is not interrupted by the use of the tongue. The goal is a fluent, flexible, and independently controlled vibrato.

Every time we pick up the oboe we must consciously recall and project the sensations which produce a simple, efficient, and pleasant tone. If there is audible distortion or if the tone does not feel open, easy, and strong, some disturbing elements (muscular tension, for example) have been unnecessarily added. These must be identified and corrected.

Curiously enough, once this concept of tone production is accepted and established, it seems ridiculous that it ever seemed difficult. The barriers that we unwittingly set up against it usually persist only because we are unaware of their existence. Sometimes the process of eliminating incorrect habits takes a long time, but the results are most rewarding.

We must keep in mind a distinction between the end we desire, that is, a satisfying musical experience, and the means we employ to gain this end. Only then can we devote critical attention to the means of performance and make a valid judgment regarding them. When we concentrate upon the musical or aesthetic results we are likely to be involved emotionally. This confuses our evaluation of cause and effect.

Summary

The benefits of proper practice are apparent only after long periods of time. It is important to set aside a regular daily practice time. A reasonable division of the available time is one-third for warmup and scales, one-third for etudes emphasizing specific technical problems, and the balance devoted to solo pieces and orchestral studies.

A methodical and objective attitude is necessary to get the most from practicing. Try mentally to "hear" each note or group of notes before they are transformed into sound. There is the danger of forming a short circuit between the printed page and the instrument unless we continually exert our precious prerogative to re-create the music mentally before it actually sounds. Conscious, creative projection of musical ideas helps keep technical habits our slaves instead of letting them become our masters.

Practice Devices

Humming

Humming while sustaining the tone helps to open the throat. Although it neither feels nor sounds good, it does open and relax tone production. If it seems difficult to do at first, try it gently and be sure that the chin is "tucked in" to protect the throat. The ability to hum easily signifies that it is not needed. Difficulty in doing it may indicate undesirable tension in the throat muscles.

Exhaling through the nose

Exhaling through the nose while playing is another device for opening up the tone production. The throat must be relaxed before the valve regulating the flow of air into the nose can open. This trick is useful in several ways. It tends to release unnecessary tension, it helps to get rid of excess air before taking a breath, and it can be done simultaneously with articulation to make sure that the air pressure in the mouth is being correctly sustained. The accompanying sound of escaping air, however, is unpleasant and must not be heard.

Double and triple tonguing

Double tonguing on the oboe is difficult to perform. It is worth cultivating, however, because it can be very effective. Practice it slowly and with soft syllables, seeking a sensation as far forward in the mouth as possible. Make the Ta-Ka-Ta-Ka or Da-Ga-Da-Ga evenly spaced and *legato*. Do not try for speed, especially at first, but try rather for smoothness, regularity, and ease. Learn to "speak" passages that would profit from this kind of tonguing, and gain the necessary fluency with various rhythms, so that the accent falls sometimes on the Da, other times on the Ga. Triplets may be handled by merely superimposing an accent with the breath—D̆a-Ga-Da Ğa-Da-Ga D̆a-Ga-Da Ğa-Da-Ga, etc.

Taking a breath while playing

The "glass blower's trick" is another useful device. While a lifesaver on certain occasions, it must be handled with discretion. It is accomplished in the following manner: with the throat closed, the cheeks and the tongue expel part of the air in the mouth. During the short interval that the tone is thus sustained, breath is taken in through the nose to replenish the supply in the lungs. When this device is alternated with normal blowing, a tone may be sustained indefinitely with complete control of dynamics, pitch, and most kinds of articulation. Of itself, however, it is quite unmusical, and must not be used too often. The quality of tone is uneven and the natural phrasing associated with normal breathing is lost. Avoiding a breath may be musically worse than having to make an event of taking a breath.

If you have never tried this trick, you will have to experiment a bit to acquire the feeling. Try puffing your cheeks as full of air as possible while breathing in and out normally through the nose. You will find it possible to squeeze the air in the mouth out through the lips with the cheek muscles or by pushing forward with the back of the tongue. The normal breath source is not used at all. It takes only a little experimentation and practice to take a breath in through the nose while expelling air through the mouth.

Silent practice

Silent practice is a useful device because:

1. It encourages an active projection of the sound in the player's mind instead of through the instrument.

2. It focuses attention on the rhythm and steadiness of the finger technique.

3. It provides needed rest for the embouchure if alternated with regular practicing.

The English Horn

As far as playing principles are concerned, the English horn is identical to the oboe. First, cultivate a feeling for tone production, then cultivate control without distortion. It is interesting to note that, because of the deeper tone and lower pitch, practicing the English horn actually helps to strengthen a feeling for oboe tone. The larger English horn reed, being easier to manage, does have a tendency to make the embouchure temporarily less sensitive to the oboe reed, but the benefits derived from playing this instrument are lasting, and in the long run outweigh this disadvantage.

Careful consideration should be given to the selection and maintenance of English horn equipment. The addition of the bocal affords another place for air to leak out unless the reed fits snugly. The bocal should be well matched to the instrument. Its length and bore will not only affect the pitch but will also influence the quality and stability of the tone. Several bocals should be tested to determine the one best suited to the around both upper and lower blades, and the tongue should rest close under the lower corner of the reed.

English Horn Adjusting Mechanism

Adjusting Screws *#1* and *2* regulate the height of the octave key pads.

Screw *#3* With the second finger of the left hand down, observe the C pad (between 1st and 2nd fingers of left hand) as the 1st finger of the right hand is put down. If the pad raises even slightly, #3 should be tightened (turned clockwise). If it is too tight, excessive finger pressure will be necessary to press the A key. Check this adjustment with cigarette paper.

#4 regulates the height of the B♭ and the C♮ pads. If it is too tight, the B♭ pad (between 2nd and 3rd fingers) will stand open.

#5 If too loose, will permit the B♭ pad to open slightly when the G key and the F♯ key are closed. If too tight, the G key pad will require excessive pressure to close.

#6 Co-ordinates the closing of the A resonance pad. If it is too tight, the G pad will not readily close. If too loose, the resonance pad will leak.

#7 regulates the height of the G♯ pad.

#8 regulates the closing of a pad necessary for notes below F♯. If it is too tight, the E and D keys may not cover. If it is too loose, air will leak by the pad.

#9 and *10* regulate the balance between the E and D keys, so that the pad referred to in #8 will be equally and separately controlled by the E and D keys.

#11, 12 and *13* all regulate the forked F resonance pad. This pad stands open for notes above E. First, adjust #12 so that the low C♮ key will just barely close the resonance pad. Then regulate screws 11 and 13 so that when *both* E and D keys are closed, the resonance pad will also *just* close.

#14 regulates the closing of the E♭ pad by the C♮ and C♯ keys.

#15 regulates the opening of the E♭ pad by the left-hand E♭ key.

#16 regulates the closing of the C♯ pad when the low B key is used.

The resonance of some notes may be improved by slight changes of fingering from that of the oboe. The E (concert pitch A) is likely to be sharp on the English horn. If no compensation for this is made, the whole instrument is

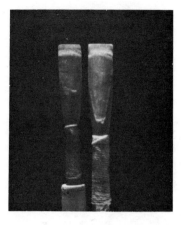

ILLUSTRATION 11   Oboe and English horn reeds

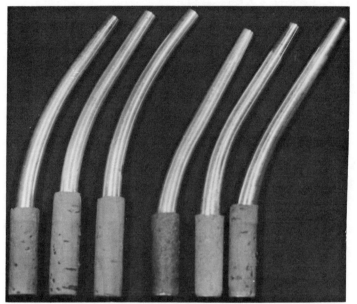

Lorée			Rigoutat			
1	**2**	**3**	**4**	**5**	**6**	
.123	.123	.123	.123	.123	.123	Top inside diameter (in inches)
.242	.240	.235	.225	.225	.225	Bottom inside diameter (in inches)
89	90	91	85	87	90	Approximate length (in millimeters)

ILLUSTRATION 12   English horn bocals

instrument. The B, C, and C♯ in the middle register are most likely to suffer. These notes may sag when a *diminuendo* is made, even when proper support is maintained. Another important factor is the amount of curve in the bocal. If it places the reed on the lip almost horizontally, the bocal should be straightened somewhat. As with the oboe, the lips should be equally placed

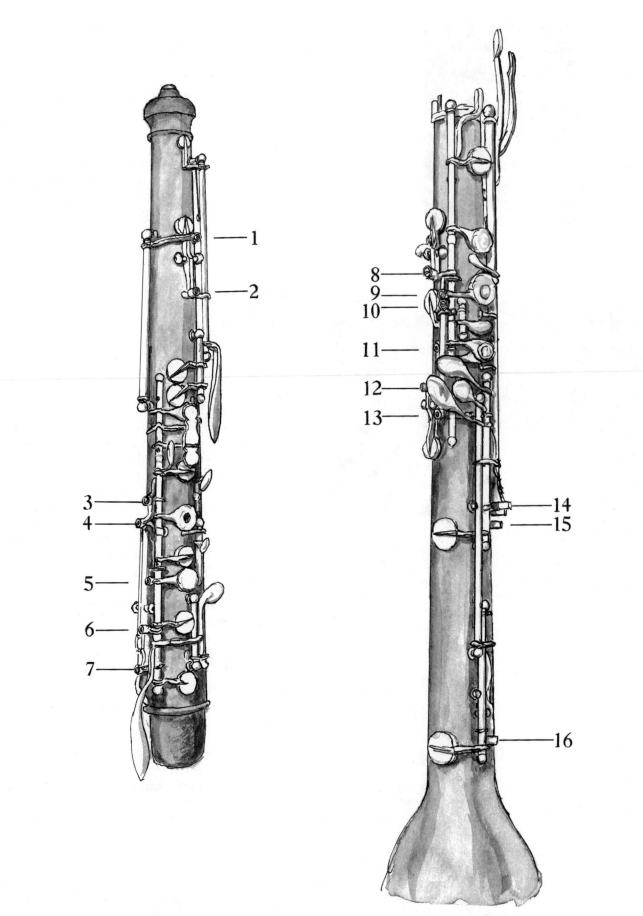

ILLUSTRATION 13

34

liable to be tuned too low. Holding down the left hand E♭ key will often lower the E the right amount. In any case, instead of tuning the instrument only to the E, more attention should be given to the tuning of the other notes. The addition of the low B key helps to stabilize notes from E′ up through G′. The A′ may be benefited by holding down the low D or E keys. The B♭′ is improved by adding the E and C keys, and it is convenient then to slur smoothly to C′, C♯′, and D′. Keeping down both the E and C keys serves to steady the instrument and to stabilize the tone.

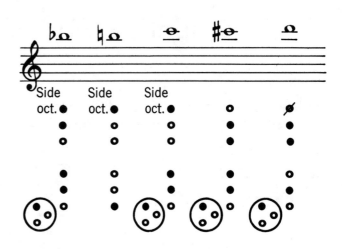

EXAMPLE 6

Fingering and Trill Fingering Chart

Only the less obvious trills are shown on this chart. Some of the trill fingerings are impossible unless the instrument has the indicated keys. Arrows indicate finger(s) to be moved for the trill.

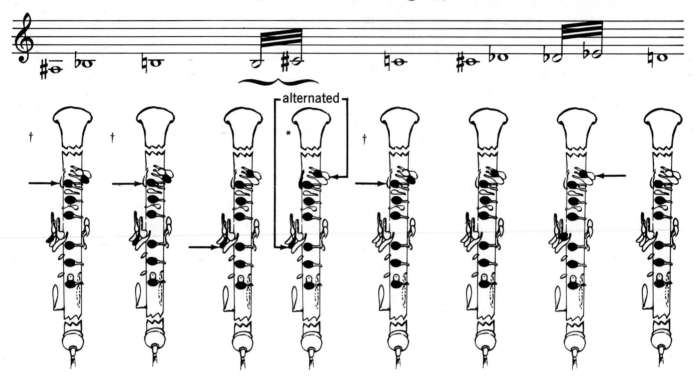

† auxiliary C key may be substituted for the right little finger.   * if oboe does not have articulated B-C# keys.

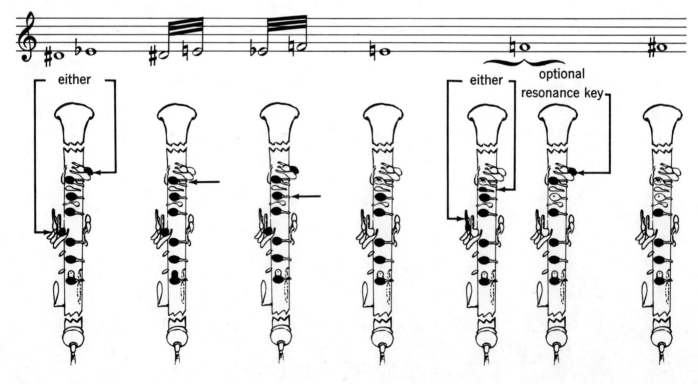

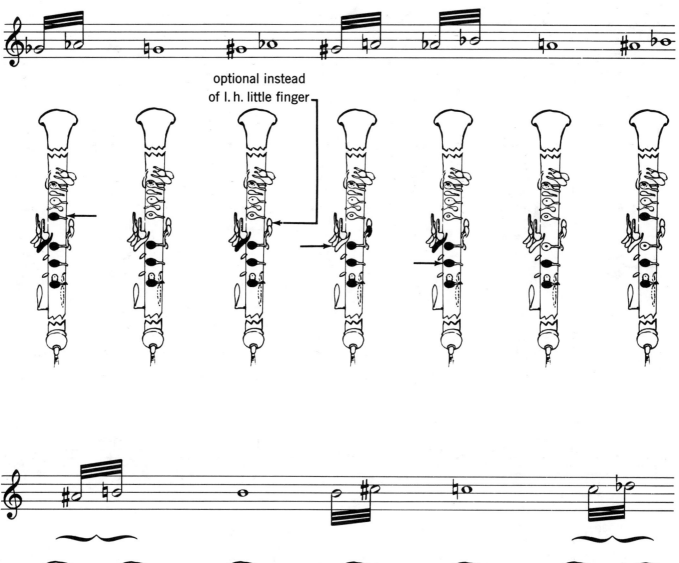

optional instead
of l. h. little finger

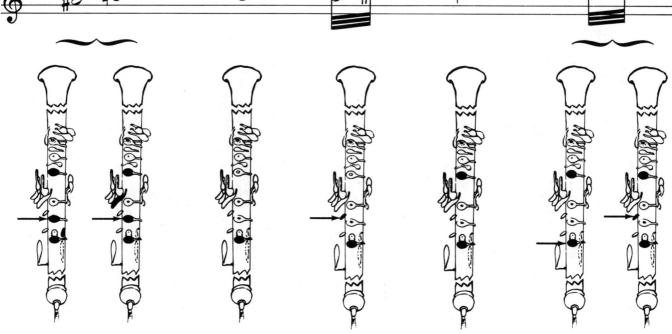

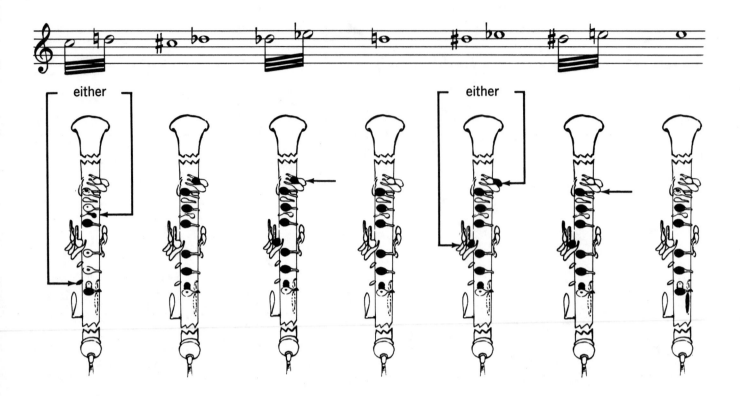

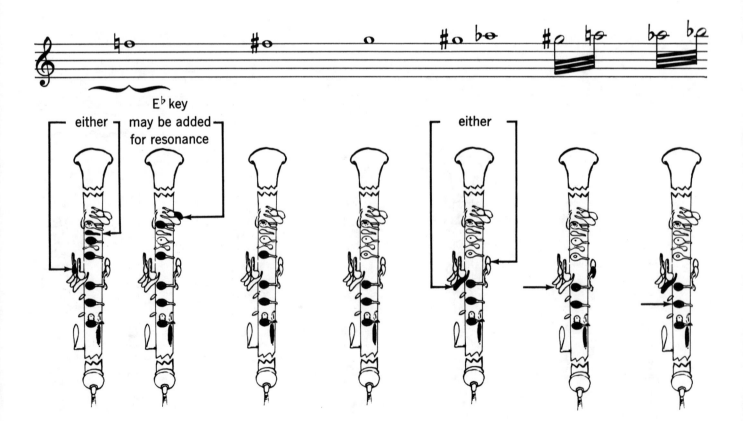

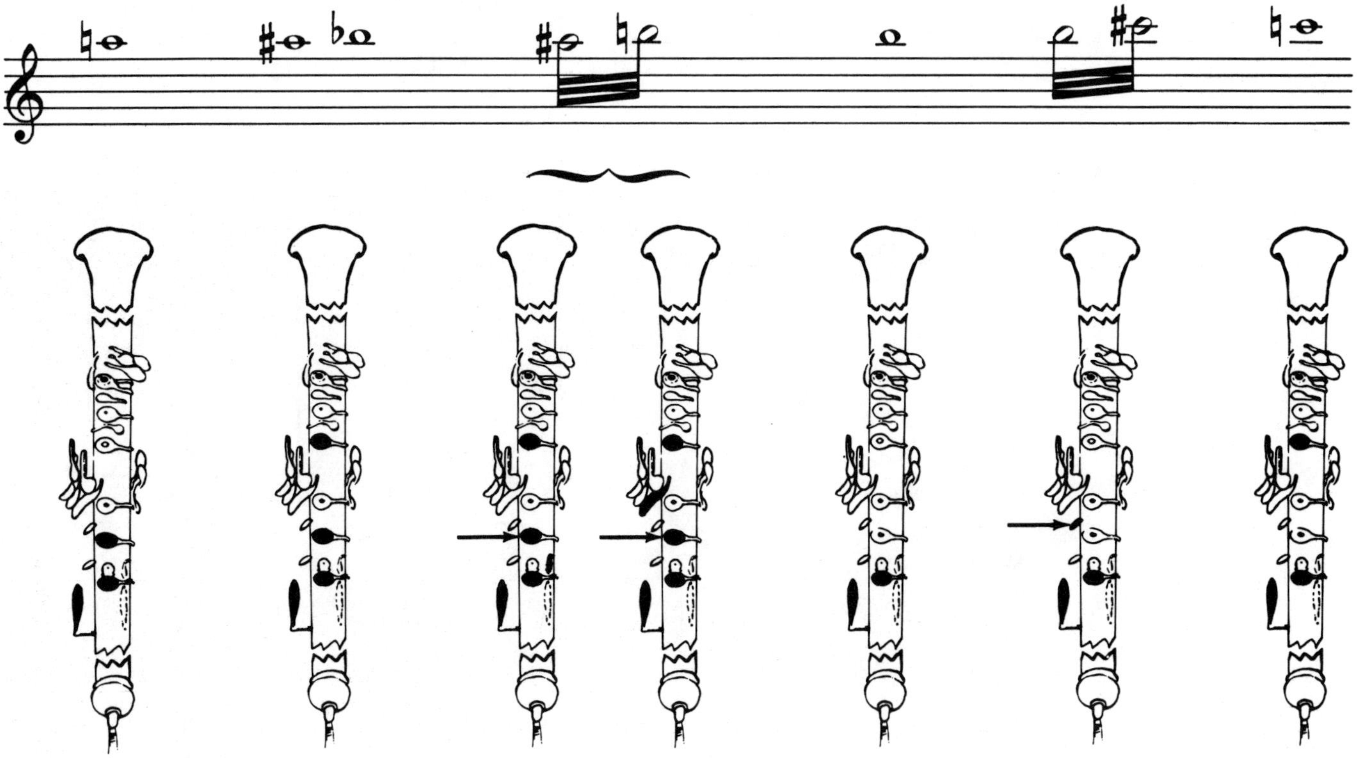

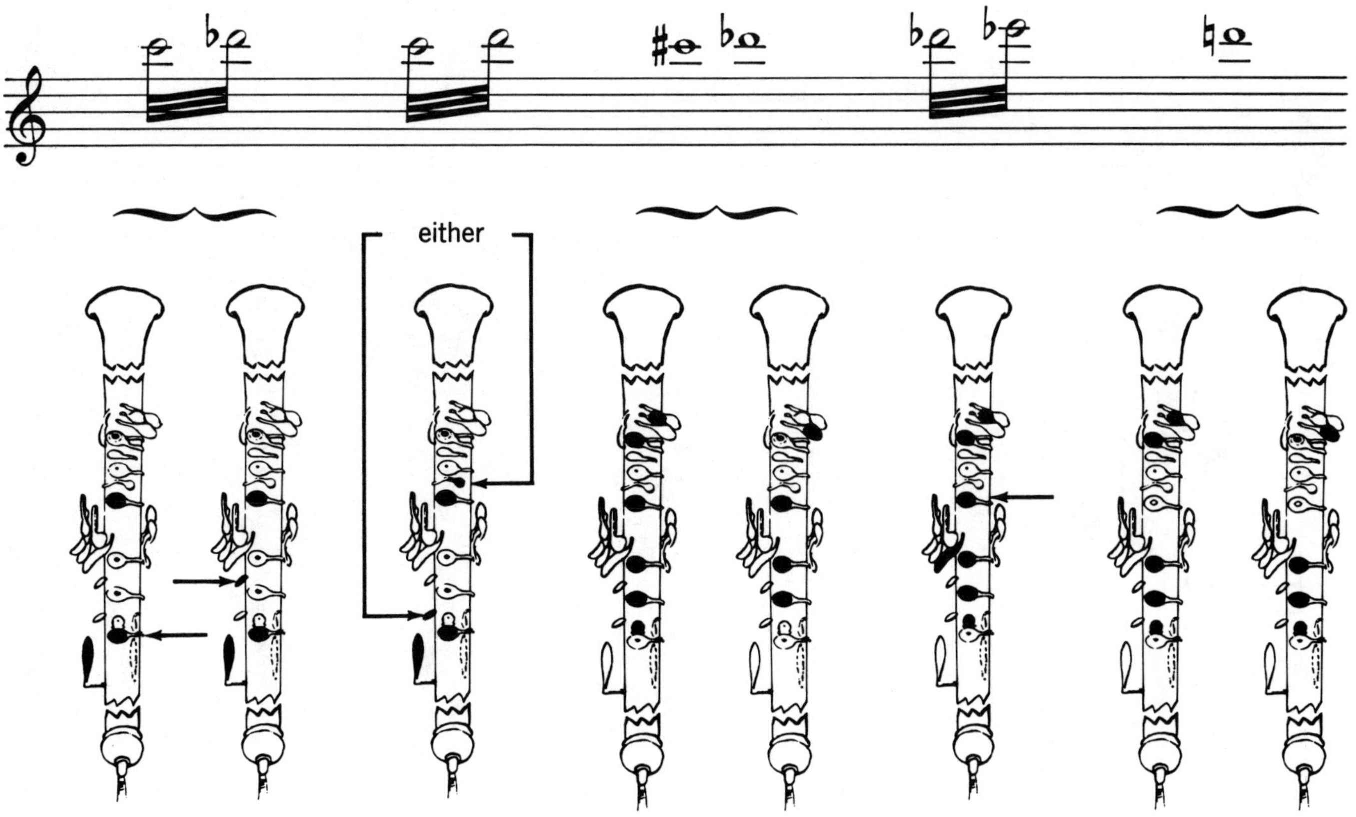
either

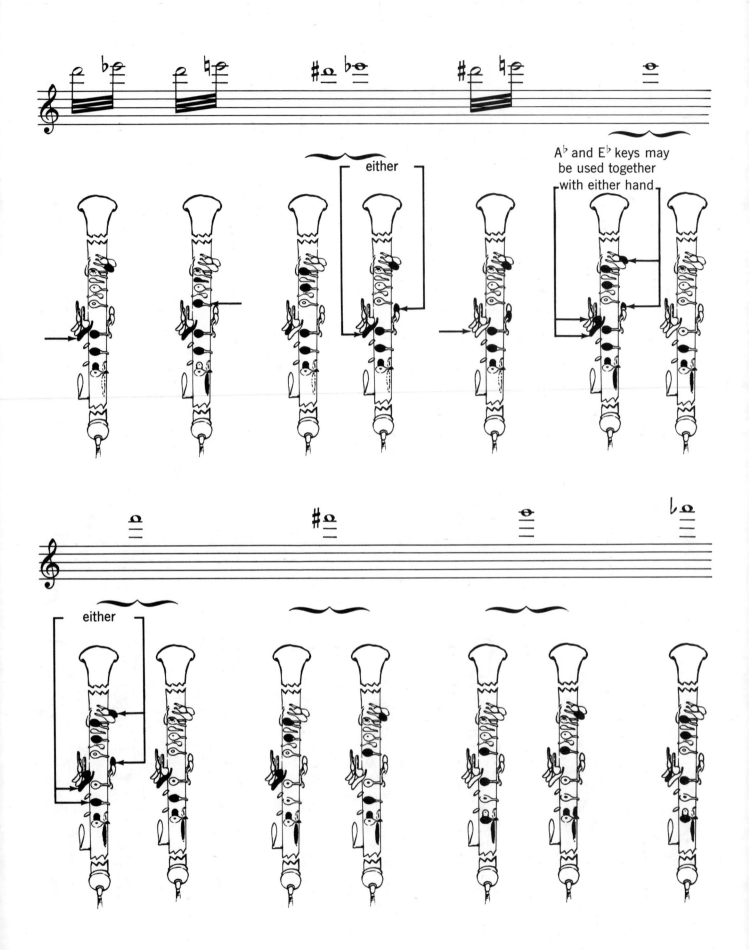

Problems and Techniques of Oboe Reedmaking

From the standpoint of both the teacher and the student, reedmaking is a most important aspect in the pedagogy of the instrument. Over ninety per cent of the world's great oboists feel that reedmaking and successful playing are inseparable. Only a few fine oboists do not make their own reeds completely, and even they do their own adjusting.

There are several reasons why making one's reeds is so important to successful playing:

1. An oboist's playing style is largely dictated by his choice of reed. Articulation, breathing, flexibility, and intonation are affected by the particular reed. It is to the oboist's advantage to be able to control the reed factors which make for better playing.
2. The oboist's aural concept of his tonal quality is successfully achieved largely by his choice of reed.
3. Variation of quality and pitch in oboes makes it necessary for the student to make a reed that will complement his particular instrument.
4. Physical characteristics of players temper tonal results. Thus, having an individualized reed is imperative for the person who wishes to closely suit his embouchure and other physical characteristics to his reed.
5. The impermanent nature of reeds makes it necessary to constantly replenish the supply.
6. Commercial reeds seldom, if ever, suit to the fullest extent the individual needs of the player. Inadequate as some may be, they do serve the purpose of supplying something for a beginner to use until he can make or finish his own reeds.

The objective of oboe reedmaking for most oboists is, of course, to provide them with a sound-producing agent which will balance their instrument, embouchure, breath pressure, playing needs, and fulfill their aural concept of how an oboe should sound.

Because the above-named factors vary, several types of reed scrapes have evolved which suit individual needs and preferences. It should be recognized that there is *no one correct way* to scrape a reed. An extensive study of reeds of many of the foremost players from all over the world shows that the methods and techniques described here closely follow universally-accepted procedures. The reed styles described and photographs used in the scraping process are examples of a school of reedmaking representative of a type of sound prevalent in the United States. This sound has achieved almost general acceptance in virtually every ranking orchestra in the country during the past twenty years.

Many of the fundamental principles of reedmaking are the same regardless of the particular school of playing or style of scrape. All aspiring reedmakers must learn to use certain materials and learn certain introductory operations. For example, it is necessary for all reedmakers to learn to use a knife, plaque, and mandrel; to learn about the gouging and shaping of cane; and to learn a method of binding the cane on the staple.

The beginning reedmaker, having little or no basis in experience, has more success at first if he has a set of definite, tested methods to follow. It is true that there are "many roads to Rome." However, in order to get there in a reasonable time, it is advantageous to be directed along a definite route. Variation of style can easily be developed after a person has acquired some basis for judgment.

It is generally best for the beginning oboist to start reedmaking only after he has played awhile, so he will not be burdened with the reed problem until he has learned something about the rudiments of music, embouchure, breathing, tonguing, and finger technique. During this first year or two the beginner may play on commercial reeds or reeds made for him by his teacher. If the oboist is a youngster, he may have to wait even longer before beginning to make his own reeds. There are, of course, exceptions to the rule. The writer knows several talented sixth-graders who make very good reeds.

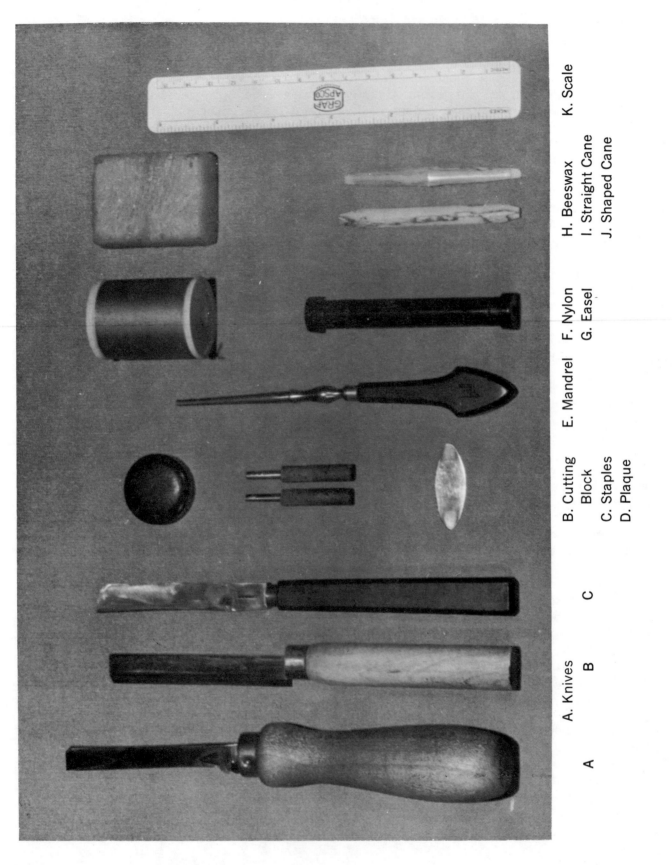

A. Knives

A   B   C

B. Cutting   E. Mandrel   F. Nylon   H. Beeswax   K. Scale
     Block   G. Easel   I. Straight Cane
C. Staples   J. Shaped Cane
D. Plaque

ILLUSTRATION 14

Standard Reedmaking Tools

Certain basic tools are required for making oboe reeds. They are few in number, and with use will pay for themselves many times over. These may be specialized tools or standard tools modified to suit the reedmaker's use. Some of the necessary items can be obtained at hardware stores, drug stores, etc., but the specialized materials must be obtained from a dealer, repairman, or supply house that handles oboe reedmaking tools. The enterprising person can make tools such as the plaque, knife, or wooden cutting block provided a good model is used.

All the tools necessary for the beginning reedmaker are shown in Illust. 14. If the beginner uses cane that is already shaped, articles G and H will not be necessary. They are used in conjunction with a shaper as shown in Illust. 40.

Following is a list of basic tools arranged so that those necessary for a beginner head the list. Since some reedmakers have refinements of their own, remarks are made explaining the various uses and functions of each tool. The tools necessary for gouging and shaping will be discussed later in the book.

Knife

A reedmaker usually has a preference for certain styles of knives because he feels that the best results can be achieved with a blade of a particular shape or weight. The blade styles used most frequently are shown in Illust. 15. The entire blades and handles can be seen in Illust. 14.

Knife A (Illust. 15) has a blade 3″ x 1/8″ x 1/2″ with approximately 1/8″ (or 90°) taper to an edge. The handle is 3-3/4″ x 1/2″ x 11/16″. Two factors which recommend this knife type are the rather heavy blade and the hardness of the steel. A well-tempered piece of steel will hold an edge longer than a soft piece. Some reedmakers feel

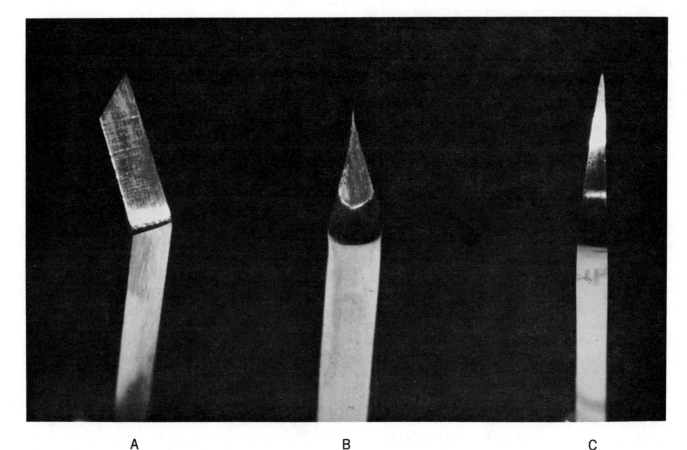

A   B   C

ILLUSTRATION 15   Knife Blades

that the heavy blade will take off more wood or bark with less "chatter" of the blade and with fewer nicks in the cane than will a light blade. In the final analysis, this is a result of the individual reedmaker's knife technique. When surveying reeds of many oboists, the reader will see that they are all products of an individual knife technique. This is one of the most important techniques for the student reedmaker to acquire, and it will personalize his reeds just as brush strokes on a painter's canvas characterize the artist. The writer recommends using the knife rather leisurely and deliberately.

Knife B (Illust. 15) is a straight razor blade that has been ground down to where the "V" starts. This grinding cuts off the thin part of the blade that will "chatter" if left on. Straight razors are made in many weights and shapes; therefore, no definite dimensions can be given except to say that an average blade is approximately 3″ long, and after grinding is approximately 1/2″ in height. Honing will gradually reduce this 1/2″ so the blade will be less hollow ground. Heavy and light straight razors can be found and then ground on a home grinder or by a local scissors grinder. Old razors can usually be purchased for a nominal price from a barber shop. Extreme care should be used when grinding so the temper will not be taken out of the blade. This is easily done with a straight razor blade because the edge is so thin that heat is not quickly dissipated. Therefore, the edge reaches the burning point quickly. The blade can then be mounted in a file handle obtained from a hardware store. The writer prefers a large handle as shown in Illust. 14, approximately 4-1/4″ x 1-1/8″, because it fits the hand better, thus giving more control over the blade. Also, the hand does not have a tendency to cramp when working for longer periods of time as so often happens when the handle is too small for the hand. This is a small point, however, because the writer has observed talented reedmakers with fine techniques turn out excellent reeds in a short time with what seemed to be very primitive equipment.

The standard French reed knife is shown in Illust. 15c. The blade is 3″ x 7/16″ x 3/32″ and is wedged (that is, not hollow ground). The handle is 4″ x 5/8″ x 3/8″. Other types of knives are used, such as the folding jack-knife type, those resembling a paring knife, and variations of knife A in Illust. 15.

The writer has a set of four straight razor knives of graduated weights that are useful at times for scraping certain areas of the cane. He finds that, for himself, he prefers a lighter blade for scraping the tip than for the back; however, either knife A or B in Illust. 15 is a good all-purpose knife.

Fine jeweler's files, flat and round, are used by some reedmakers to take wood from certain areas of the cane. Few oboists use files, but it is common for the bassoonist to use them. For those not practiced in the art of using a file, it is difficult to take cane from a minute area, and also hard to tell exactly how much cane is being removed. In many respects, because of the size of the reed, oboe reedmaking is more critical and more meticulous and requires a greater amount of control of the variable factors than does bassoon reedmaking.

Sometimes very fine abrasive paper, *000* or *0000* polishing paper, is useful in smoothing certain areas of the cane or in taking a small bit of wood from the edge of the tip of the reed. Dutch rush can be used, but it is more practical for adjusting clarinet reeds.

It is possible to put a preliminary lay on a reed by using a slowly turning, horizontal grindstone. This practice is not recommended for the beginner.

Sharpening the Knife

The writer wishes to emphasize that the knife must be sharp at all times. Scraping with different portions of the blade can be managed by sliding the top of the knife along the left thumb when the knife is held in position for scraping (Illust. 35 and 36). This movement exposes a different section of the knife edge to the cane. When areas of the knife edge become dull, the degree of dullness can be detected by holding the edge so that light can reflect on the dull places along the edge, or by feeling with the thumb, or by gently drawing the edge across the thumbnail. When the thumbnail test is used, the blade will slide across the dull areas and the sharp areas will dig in, causing intermittent jerks which can be felt. Of course, the best test is simply that the knife will not cut cane but will tend to tear and pull the fibers off rather than to cut or scrape cleanly. A piece of cane which is too wet will have almost the same result. When cane does not cut well, either because of a dull knife or cane that is too wet, the reedmaker must push and gouge with the blade. If he pushes downward too hard with the blade or with the left thumb, he will pull areas of the tip off the reed and, in general, turn out a primitive-looking and unbalanced reed. When the knife is sharp, the edge cannot be seen when held up to the light for reflection; it will feel sharp to the thumb; it will cut or scrape the cane cleanly if the cane is not too wet or pithy; and it will easily shave the hair from the back of the hand. Stropping the blade puts too fine an edge on the knife.

The writer has used many types of sharpening stones and finds a Carborundum (Fine, 8" x 2" x 3/4") the best general-purpose stone. It is man-made, in contrast to natural stones such as India, soapstone, or Hard Arkansas. A size smaller than the one given above is not recommended because too little of the knife blade comes in contact with the stone at one time. The fine grade seems to cut just enough steel to sharpen an edge in a reasonable time. Coarse stone cuts too fast and hones away the knife too quickly; however, coarse-grade abrasive is helpful in other operations, such as in the early or rough honing of the blade preparatory to finishing it with a finer stone. In this operation a coarse grade can save considerable time, but it will never put the necessary fine edge on the knife.

A small oilcan filled with number ten motor oil or "Pike Oil" will aid in the sharpening process. Oils that become gummy are not recommended. Some reedmakers use water instead of oil, depending upon the stone. The oil keeps the pores of the stone from clogging with minute steel shavings that are cut from the blade as well as keeping these small shavings wet and washing about in the pores of the stone. This makes them part of the abrasive surface. A dirty stone is an inefficient cutting agent and should be cleaned with soap and water or kerosene; however, with average use and turned regularly and oiled properly, it will be years before a cleaning is necessary.

Several methods of sharpening which insure good results will be discussed. For any hollow ground or flat surface, except the French knife (C in Illust. 15), oil should be put on the stone and the knife should be placed on the stone as shown in Illust. 16.

The knife should be pushed with the edge away from the body, blade flat, up to the end of the stone, moving the blade across the stone from left to right, or from the heel of the blade to the tip of the blade. This one stroke covers the entire blade. Downward pressure is maintained during the stroke with the left thumb or the fingers on the tip end of the blade and with the same pressure from the right hand holding the handle. Next, the edge is turned toward the body, the heel of the blade is shifted to the edge

of the stone, moving to the left, and the blade is pulled flat across the stone, thereby completing an "X" pattern (Illust. 16 and 17).

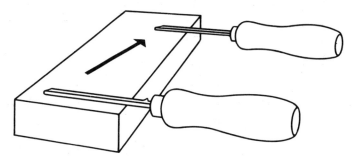

ILLUSTRATION 16

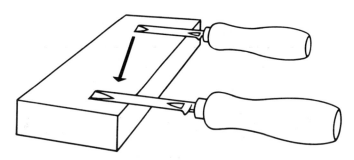

ILLUSTRATION 17

The last stroke, always against the edge, should be made pushing away from the body, thus turning the minute burr of the edge so that it will catch the cane better. The "X" pattern is used because (under magnification) it forms the saw-teeth of the blade in the shape of a "Λ." If the blade is pushed and drawn always in the same manner (⟋ or ⟍), the teeth will be turned in those directions.

Hollow ground blades may also be sharpened with a circular motion (Illust. 18), or by making a figure eight motion (Illust. 19).

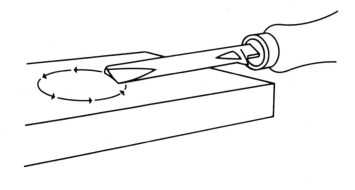

ILLUSTRATION 18

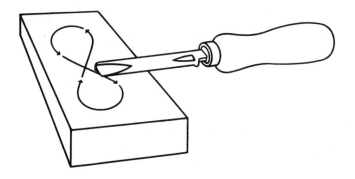

ILLUSTRATION 19

To sharpen a knife with the characteristics of that shown in Illust. 15a, the following (Illust. 20a and b) should be used as a reference.

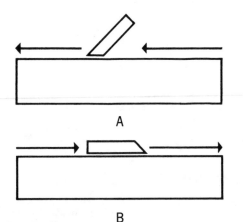

A

B

ILLUSTRATION 20

When the small surface is sharpened as in 20a above, great care should be taken not to tilt the blade up on edge. After making a few passes (straight, circular, or figure eight) on the small surface, covering the entire blade, the blade should be turned flat on its back and honed. This process is repeated until the edge is sharp.

The writer has found only two ways to effectively sharpen the French-style knife (Illust. 15c). The first is to draw it across the plaque, cleaning and sharpening the blade at the same time. The other is to tilt the blade up on edge slightly when pushing or drawing across the stone. If the edge is not tilted, the sharpening process is interminable since so much metal must be cut from the blade (a difficulty never encountered with a hollow ground blade). *Remove all oil* from the knife blade and fingers before working on cane.

Plaque

The plaque (Illust. 14d) is 1-3/8″ long, 1/2″ wide and is cut from blued spring steel .27 mm. thick (which is fairly standard). Some reedmakers prefer a narrower plaque than this; then the knife does not come in contact with the sides of the plaque as much when scraping the sides of the cane, and the knife edge is not dulled. Softer materials can be used for a plaque, but are not satisfactory because the substance wears or gets scraped into the tip of the reed. The light color of the cane shows up well against the blue of the steel, and the tip and lay can be seen better after the plaque is inserted. The use of the plaque is shown in Illust. 54 and 55.

Mandrel

This tool is elliptical on the end, gradually becoming circular approximately 45 to 50 mm. from the large end. When inserted into the staple, the outside of the mandrel should fit the inside of the staple exactly. The uses of the mandrel when inserted in the staple are as follows:

1. The handle is a guide for putting the cane on the staple squarely across the elliptical end of the staple.

2. The mandrel will not allow the metal tube to crush inward under the pressure of the nylon binding.

3. The mandrel helps hold the reed while it is being bound and scraped.

Some reedmakers maintain that the mandrel and staples need not match, and make good reeds to prove it, but the writer feels that it is an advantage if the two match. When the mandrel fits, staple adjustments can be made without damaging the staples (Illust. 59-62). When, after experimentation, the correct dimension staple and mandrel are found, they can serve as a dimension check for other staples. Mandrels and staples from the same maker will usually fit each other well. When the oboist uses a mandrel with staples from another maker there is likely to be a slight difference of fit.

Staples

Present-day staples (Illust. 14c) are made of brass or nickel silver by forming the metal around a mandrel and sealing the seam or are built up by electro-deposition. Most staples are of the former type. The writer recommends that the beginner use staples 47 mm. in length. Any deviations should probably be shorter rather than longer. When the player has gained experience in reedmaking he may desire to use a different dimension staple to aid the pitch level, response, or intonation of his instrument.

Cutting Block

The small block (Illust. 14b) is approximately 25 mm. in diameter and 10 mm. high. The top, or cutting surface, is slightly curved and the bottom is flat. It is used to trim the tip of a reed as shown in Illust. 56. The writer has seen larger and differently shaped blocks than the one pictured, but never a smaller one. Regardless of the size, they all have the common cutting surface for trimming the reed tip. Some reedmakers prefer the rounded surface; others prefer a surface that is almost flat. Over a period of time, depending upon how much cutting is done, the surface of the block will become crosshatched with knife marks. From time to time these marks should be scraped off so that the surface remains clean and even.

Nylon and Beeswax

These are used in the binding of the cane onto the staple (Illust. 14f and h). Before nylon was manufactured, silk thread was used. Silk has one advantage over nylon; it is softer and the individual turns around the cane tend to spread together more. This stops some of the leaks that sometimes occur in this area when the turns are not tight against each other. Nylon is strong and when coated with a bit of beeswax becomes even stronger. The thread is drawn over the beeswax two or three times while being held into the wax with the left thumb. The wax seals the cracks between the turns much as silk does. If too much wax is put on the thread, it becomes saturated and breaks easily. Some reedmakers do not use beeswax. Instead, they paint the binding with clear fingernail polish. A block of beeswax, approximately 1-1/2″ x 2″ x 3/4″, can be purchased at most drug stores and should last for several years.

Most reedmakers use nylon instead of silk. The larger the thread, the more the sides of the cane are drawn together per turn around the staple. Size twenty nylon is good for strength and for control of the sides of the reed. It can be bought in many colors in the large 1/5 lb. spindle or in regular sewing size spools. Using different colored threads will help to identify reeds made at a certain time, from a particular batch of cane, or from a particular dimension of gouge. If a large quantity is bought, it must be wrapped on a holder of some sort (Illust. 14f) so the reedmaker can pull it tight. The tautness required may cause the thread to cut the skin if one tries to bind cane on the staple while holding the single strand of nylon in the bare hand. If the smaller spools are used (a good way to vary colors), the spool itself becomes a fine holder. Size twenty nylon thread can be obtained from department stores, fabric shops, mills, or from anyone who handles reedmaking supplies.

Cane

Cane which is gouged only, or both gouged and shaped, can be purchased from firms who handle reedmaking supplies. The beginner should purchase preshaped cane from reputable sources. This cuts down the number of operations and the number of tools required at the outset. Later on, the oboist may wish to split and gouge his own cane from the tube and shape it on the shaper of his choice. Another method is to purchase and shape straight, gouged cane.

Scale

The writer prefers a scale of the type shown in Illust. 14k because it is calibrated in both inches and millimeters. The figures and marks are black on a white background for better visibility, while the size is such that it is not awkward to use. This scale is obtainable at any stationer's store.

Easel

This circular piece of hardwood is used to hold the straight, gouged cane in order to mark it for bending and also for trimming the ends before shaping (Illust. 35 and 36). Easels of different makers vary slightly in dimension. Illust. 14g is 87 mm. long and 12 mm. in diameter. The inside length which holds the cane is 77 mm. with a mark around the exact center.

The Gouging Process

The first step in the gouging process is splitting pieces from the tube of cane. These preliminary pieces are thick and must be pregouged (filièred) and then gouged to a usable thickness and contour. Consequently, the gouging process can be divided into three basic operations: splitting, pre-gouging, and gouging. Illust. 21 shows the marks for splitting, outline of pre-gouging, and an outline of two possible contours of gouging superimposed on a cross section of tube cane. The measurements in this illustration are approximate and variation is possible. Note that the center of the gouged cane is thick and the wood is graduated evenly to thinner sides. Some reedmakers prefer the thicker center ridge in the cane to extend farther out into the sides. The variations of this ridge affect the opening of the reed somewhat. This thickness in the center and graduation away from the center is variable, depending upon the contour of the gouging blade and its setting in the machine. This thickness and contour is known as the gouge of the cane. Illust. 21D and E show two possible gouged contours. It should be noted that there are other contours and also variations on those shown in the illustration. Good gouge is not a question of a "correct" measurement; it is good only when the result is a usable reed which can meet the needs and desires of the player. Fortunately, much commercial cane can be used with adequate results. In some instances the reed would function better if the gouge were more suited to the particular oboist and his equipment.

Many of the measurements described above are so minute that only the person trained to notice such detail can tell these differences in actual practice. Beyond certain limits, measurement of cane is not an asset. The scientific approach is progressively inhibited as it is overpowered by the uncontrollable nature of the cane itself.

Illust. 22 shows a series of canes in progressive stages from the tube to the final shaping, ready to bind on the staple.
The stages are:
A. Tube cane
B. One of the three segments split from the tube
C. A segment that has had one end trimmed preparatory to pre-gouging

D. Pre-gouged
E. Gouged
F. Shaped and folded

Gouge quality is an important variable to control in reedmaking. Smoothness of the gouged surface, a balanced graduation on either side of the center, and the thickness of the center itself are all most important factors. Variance of thickness of the center and the balanced gradation on either side of it will dictate the length and contour of the lay of the reed. In turn, the lay of the reed largely dictates the reed's playing response. As a general rule, the thicker the gouge, the more wood must be removed from the cane by scraping; the thinner the gouge, the less wood can be removed from the cane by scraping.

It is not known whether the gouge dictates the scrape or whether the desired scrape dictates the measurement of the gouge. It is probably a reciprocal operation; that is, one can benefit from the other, dependent upon the player's embouchure, instrument, and musical needs.

An individual oboist can compensate for a variation of gouge because he can achieve tonal balance by varying the scrape of the reed. Likewise, he can tolerate a scrape variation dependent upon the gouge. Other factors affect the gouge and scrape—mainly the natural growth of the cane itself. Little control can be exercised over this natural growth. Thorough, careful selection of cane is therefore of utmost importance, because cane is usable only within limits. If factors which are important to a good piece of cane are out of balance with each other, it will be necessary to make a variation of scrape or gouge. In some instances the cane will be unusable. Some pieces of cane are hard, some are soft, some have a thick rind (bark), and some have a thin rind. Radius variations are commonly present in the same piece of cane after it is split from the tube. Therefore, adjusting to either the inequalities of the natural growth of the cane or of the gouge and/or scrape is an important part of reedmaking which must be recognized.

The professional oboist cannot tolerate as much reed variation as the average oboist because his needs and preferences are by necessity more precise. The variations of reedmakers are great because there are many vary-

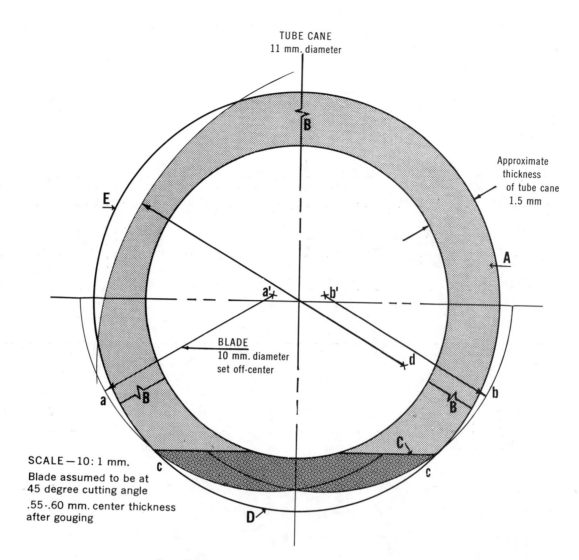

A —Tube Cane (shaded)

B —Sections split from Tube Cane

C —Outline of Cane as it comes from the tube
after pre-gouging (textured) and after gouging (untextured)

D —Outline of gouged cane (varied by shape
of blade) (untextured)

    a —contour cut by first gouging
    a′ —axis of contour **a**
    b —contour cut by reversing cane in the
        gouger bed and gouging a second time
    b′ —axis of contour **b**
    c —approximate thickness of sides
        at widest point of shape (7 mm.)

E — Outline of a gouged contour
requiring a radius of the gouge blade
larger than the radius of the tube cane
(varied by shape of blade) (white areas within cane)

    d —axis of contour **E**

ILLUSTRATION 21

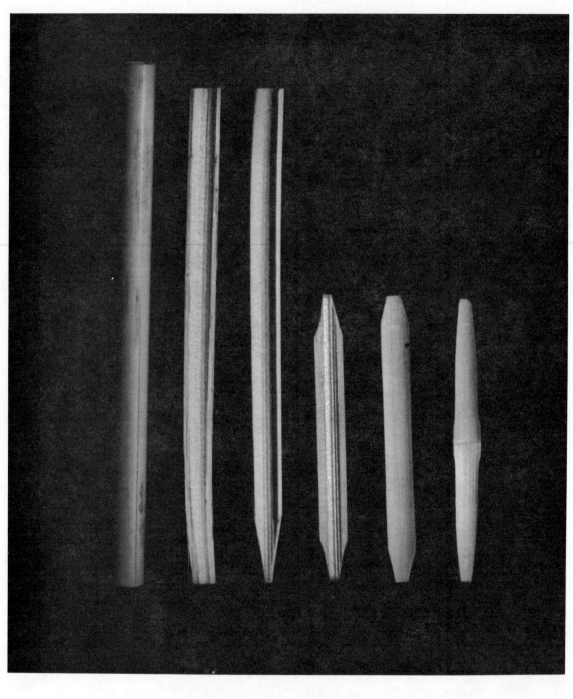

A   B   C   D   E   F

ILLUSTRATION 22

ing opinions regarding needs and preferences over the world. Yet, these players use conventional embouchures, conventional oboes, and produce an acceptable sound according to their own standards.

Florian Mueller states that Alfred Barthel (Solo Oboe, Chicago Symphony Orchestra, 1904-1929) made a very short-scrape reed by using a gouge that measured .45 mm. in the center and .45 mm on the sides. Cane gouged in this manner has no taper at all from the center of the cane to the sides; yet Barthel achieved fine results. The results of a recent check made by the writer on a piece of Mr. Barthel's cane gave the measurements of .42 mm. in the center tapering to .37 mm. on the sides. Stannard (Solo Oboe, Indianapolis Symphony Orchestra) uses cane gouged .65 mm. in the center tapering to .45 mm. on the sides. Weaver (Solo Oboe, Houston Symphony Orchestra) gouges cane .69-.71 mm. in the center tapering to .53-.56 mm. on the sides. Dandois (Solo Oboe, Cincinnati Symphony Orchestra) gouges .64 mm. in the center, and with this he makes a French-style reed. A French scrape usually requires a thinner gouge. In his latest experiments, Dandois is gouging a furrow that is .56 mm. at the center tapering to .69 mm. at each end of the piece of cane. Booth (Solo Oboe, National Symphony Orchestra, Wellington, New Zealand) gouges a furrow that tapers from .56 mm. in the center to .58 mm. on each end. Some oboists maintain that .55 mm. in the center tapering to .40 mm. on the sides is best, and the writer has had some English cane that measured .30-.35 mm. on the sides. As has been noted before, .57-.59 mm. in the center tapering to .40-.45 mm. on the sides is a good, usable average. It should be noted that reedmakers' measurements generally vary because of the measuring device used, the touch used, and variations in the cane (wet, dry, hard, soft, etc.).

When the writer measures the sides on an unshaped piece of cane, he can only approximate the distance from the center to the sides because of the lack of an instrument to measure with more accuracy. If the cane is shaped, the side measurements will vary depending upon the width of the shape at any given point.

Because of the nature of the cane, it is impossible and undesirable to control certain of the variables except within certain tolerances. For example, the measurement of gouge can vary .03 mm. between one heavy fibre (vascular bundle) on the inside of a gouge contour and the valley next to it (parenchyma). Some reedmakers minimize this by gouging cane when it is dry, thereby making the inside surface smoother. However, they keep in mind that a dry measurement is smaller than a wet one because the cane swells when wet. It is difficult, if not impossible, for the writer to tell the difference in the playing results of a finished reed whose gouge measurement varies less than .03 mm. when centered around .57 mm.

Much commercial cane has been picked over before being sold and has been gouged in a haphazard manner. The best results cannot be expected with this sort of cane. Many oboists check the gouge measurement before binding a piece of cane on a staple; this practice is an aid to consistent results. If the gouge is even in thickness, the scrape of the reeds will be more uniform. Consistency is also achieved if the individual pieces of cane closely resemble each other in texture and hardness.

Because of personal differences and preferences, the writer does not feel that the average is necessarily always the best. Certain reed styles require slightly different gouges. It is suggested that the beginner procure cane gouged between .57 and .59 mm. in the center and .40-.45 mm. on the sides, departing from this later if desirable or necessary. This measurement will suffice for almost any reed style made in the United States at the present time. Beginning reedmakers will not have enough control over the gouge of the cane used and have enough to learn at the outset without being further burdened with the gouging process. Keeping reedmaking simple is undoubtedly the best solution. Beginners must take the cane and gouge which are available from the supplier and hope that they are usable. If, after having acquired a basis for judgment, the oboist wishes to have cane gouged more to his choice, he can have it gouged to order by an expert or he can experiment with the gouging process himself.

The oboist who does not gouge his own cane has no control over the variables inherent within the gouging process. He must take the chance that the cane he buys is good cane and is properly gouged for his purpose. Many oboists do not gouge their cane because they have a source which can supply suitable gouged cane. The gouging process is time-consuming and requires experience and experimentation with the grinding and setting of the blade before the best results can be obtained.

Many oboists vary the scrape of the reed to compensate for the variance that might be present in the gouge or in the individual nature of the cane. The writer has observed, however, that these oboists usually have a supply of good well-gouged cane to begin with.

The hardness, softness, and texture of the cane will dictate to a large degree the best measurement of the gouge. Hard cane generally requires a thinner gouge than soft cane. A certain over-all type of gouge should be adopted and adhered to and varied as the need arises. A different instrument, a change of climate, a change of embouchure, a change of aural concept, or varying playing situations could result in a desirable variation of gouge.

A gouge may be termed successful if the oboist, after gouging a few pieces of cane to a particular measurement, makes a few reeds from it and gets usable results according to his style of reedmaking and his musical desires. If he cannot get the results he wants to achieve because of a gouge that is too thick or too thin in the center or on the sides, is uneven, or drops off too quickly from the center ridge, the gouge is unsuccessful.

First, select a quality piece of tube cane 10-1/2 to 11 mm. in diameter. Split the dry tube carefully with a sharp splitting tool (shown approximately twice actual size in Illust. 24 with a detail of the splitting tool shown approximately actual size in Illust. 23). Next, the length of the pre-gouger bed (Illust. 25) along the best sections of cane is approximated, with special attention to the equality of radius both around and lengthways of the tube; the edges are pared and chopped to length in the guillotine. The guillotine used for chopping cane to the length of the pre-gouger bed is shown in Illust. 26. The ends of the cane should be narrowed (Illust. 22c) to prevent splitting when using the guillotine. It may take several attempts before an inexperienced person will get the cane to fit the bed exactly. Always start with a piece of cane that is slightly too long.

The piece of dry cane is placed in the pre-gouger bed and planed across several times until no more wood will come off. Another pre-gouging method is to pull the cane through a filière, or die, which removes approximately the same amount of wood as the plane and bed type, but is awkward to use.

The cane is then soaked. The amount of soaking required will depend mainly upon the texture of the cane; four to six hours should suffice. The cane should be completely wet through its thickness, but not waterlogged. The piece of soaked

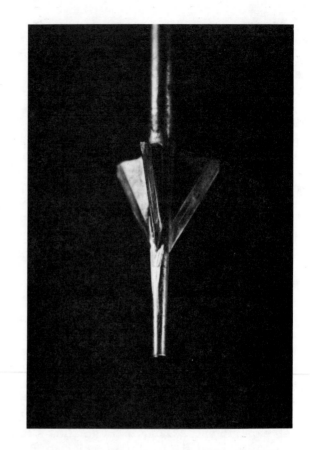

ILLUSTRATION 23   The Splitting Tool

cane is then placed in the gouging machine bed and the blade assembly put down over the cane and gouge by pushing the blade forward with an even, firm, downward pressure maintained at all times until no more wood will come off. In the hand gouging operation, the cane in the bed is usually reversed after the first gouging in order to equalize the contour on both sides of the center. Naturally, this will depend upon the shape and setting of the blade. The front view of a gouging machine is shown approximately actual size in Illust. 27. Pre-gouged cane is in the bed ready for gouging, and the assembly is tilted back to show the blade.

The blade is placed down on the cane at the right-hand end and the assembly moves from right to left, removing cane in thin slivers until no more will cut off. The setting of the blade and the bed determines the amount of wood that can be removed. Adjustments, independent of each other, can be made to move the blade and the bed up, down, or sideways. A rear view of the same machine is shown in Illust. 28.

In order to get a smoother inside surface, some reedmakers will gouge cane while it is dry. Even though this smooth surface is to be de-

(text continued on p. 62)

ILLUSTRATION 24   Splitting the Cane

ILLUSTRATION 25   The Pre-gouger

ILLUSTRATION 26   The Guillotine

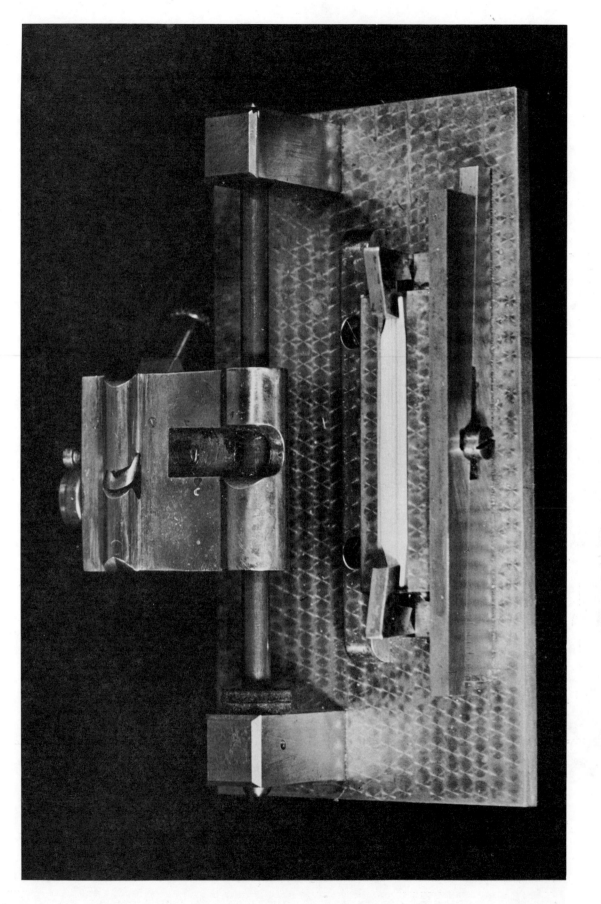

ILLUSTRATION 27   Gouging Machine—Front View

ILLUSTRATION 28   Gouging Machine — Rear View

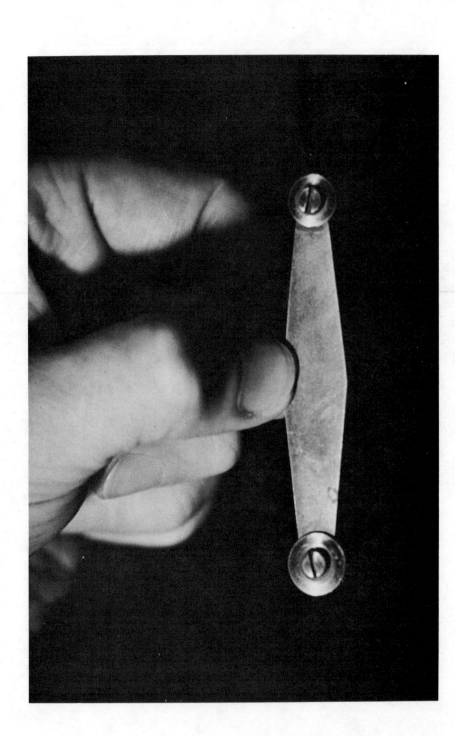

ILLUSTRATION 29   The Scraper

ILLUSTRATION 30   Micrometer

ILLUSTRATION 31   Micrometer

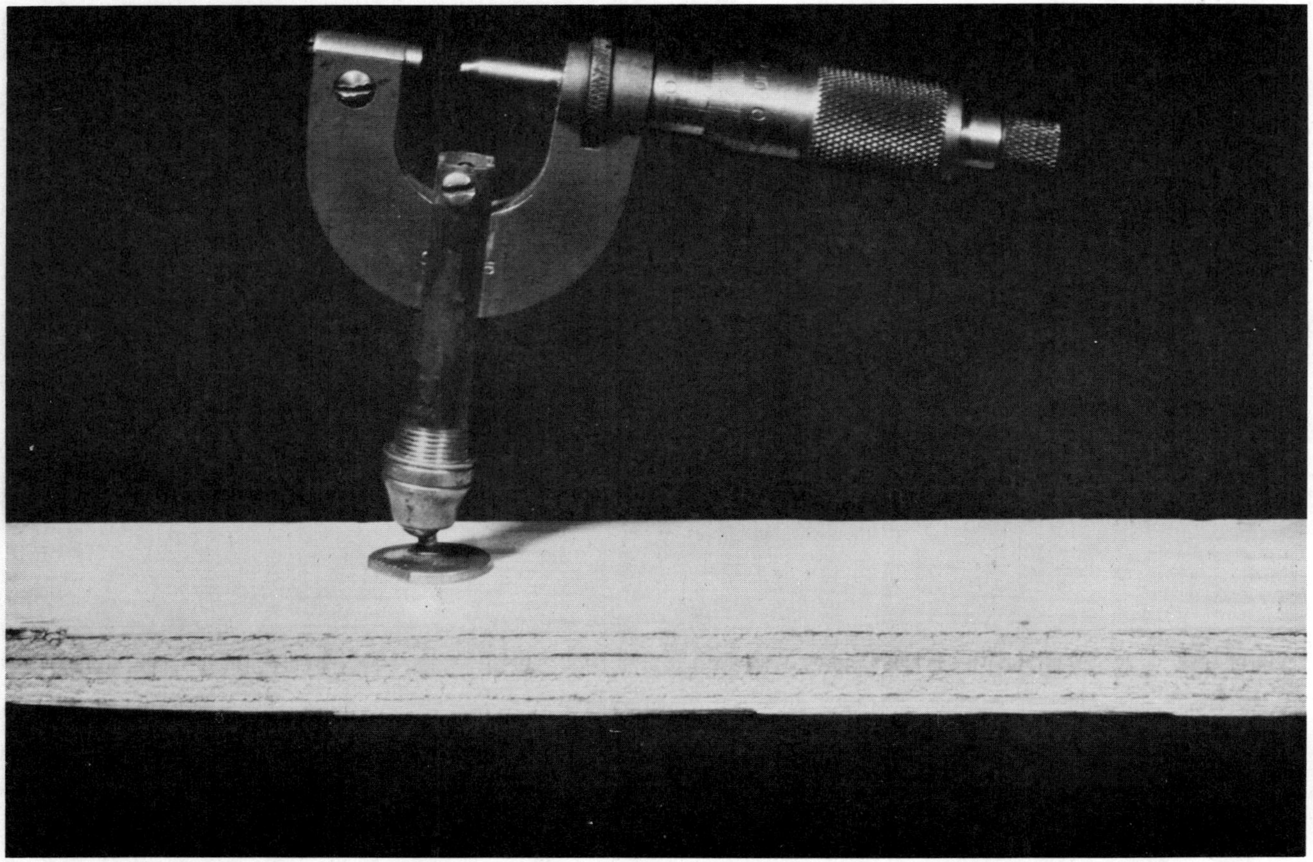

ILLUSTRATION 32   Mounted Micrometer

sired, gouging while the cane is dry dulls the blade quicker than if the cane is wet. One solution is to gouge wet cane and smooth it, if necessary, by drawing a hand scraper (Illust. 29) lightly over the contour after it dries and before it is shaped.

Just as in measuring with the micrometer, a considerable amount of the personal element is present in the gouging operation. Some practice, experimentation, and testing of the results will help to set the individual "feel" of the machine for the reedmaker. If possible, the gouging blade should be set and tested by an expert; much time can be consumed in the trial-and-error method of finding a usable measurement. After the reedmaker has had enough experience to form a basis for judgment, the trial-and-error method is valuable from an experimental standpoint.

The writer suggests that the beginner try to gouge the same measurement at first as he would ask for when buying commercially gouged cane; that is, .57-.59 mm. in the center and .40-.45 mm. on the sides. Some reedmakers use caliper-type instruments for measuring gouged cane, while others use micrometers calibrated in thousandths of an inch or in hundredths of a millimeter. A measurement any finer than the above, such as 10/1,000 of an inch, is impractical. The conversion of thousandths of an inch to hundredths of a millimeter is as follows:

.020″ = .513 mm.	.026″ = .667 mm.
.021″ = .538 mm.	.027″ = .693 mm.
.022″ = .564 mm.	.028″ = .718 mm.
.023″ = .585 mm.	.029″ = .744 mm.
.024″ = .615 mm.	.030″ = .769 mm.
.025″ = .641 mm.	

Since measurement is a comparative operation, calipers or micrometers are equally good after the reedmaker is experienced with one or the other. The writer prefers a micrometer because there is a personal contact or "feel" in the use of it. Allowances can easily be made in the touch for differently textured, wet or dry pieces of cane. The dial indicator takes most of the personal element from the measuring operation and does not allow for differences in cane texture. If two pieces of cane are the same thickness, the dial indicator (having constant spring tension) will indent a soft piece more than a hard piece and thereby record a smaller measurement on the softer piece when actually they are the same.

A micrometer of French manufacture, with the spindle ground slightly round so as to fit the curvature of the inside of the cane, is shown in

Illust. 30 (enlarged approximately four times). A micrometer of American manufacture with the spindle left a little flat is shown in Illust. 31 (enlarged approximately four times). This contour is good, if not too flat, because it will display itself over more wood surface. If used with a light touch it will not indent the wood as much as a rounded contour.

A simple method of mounting a micrometer with a ball-and-socket is shown in Illust. 32 (approximately actual size). A mounted micrometer frees both hands so that the cane may be manipulated with the left hand and the micrometer dial with the right. If an unmounted micrometer is used, the micrometer and cane are both held in the left hand and the dial is turned with the right.

A millimeter radius gauge opened to 5 and 5-1/2 mm. is shown in Illust. 33 (approximately actual size). This is the radius of a piece of tube cane 10 mm. and 11 mm. in diameter. When this tool is used to select the correct size cane tubes, any variation of radius can be seen by noting where the light shines through the crack between the tool and the tube of cane. This tool is also useful for measuring cane that has already been gouged, or gouged and shaped.

ILLUSTRATION 33 Radius Gauge

A more haphazard method of measuring cane tubes is to cut a 10-1/2 or 11 mm. slot in a piece of wood, metal, or cardboard and then using the tubes that come closest to fitting the slot. This method has some merit for preliminary selection, but gives little indication of radius variations in a single tube.

The Shaping Process

The process of shaping consists of preparing and cutting a gouged piece of cane to the size of a steel pattern or shaping tool so that it may be bound onto a staple. There is no standard shape; it is a variable used to each player's advantage. The shape can also be a detriment, affecting especially the pitch and sometimes the centering of the tone if the dimensions of the top, center, or throat portions of the shape are not properly balanced to themselves, to the staple, to the oboe, or to the embouchure.

The important parts of a shape contour are the width of the top where the tip of the reed will fall; the point of noticeable taper, which is one factor in determining the opening of the reed; and the width of the throat (the part which is immediately above the binding when the cane is bound on the staple).

Many results are achieved by varying the shape. A wider shape causes a lower pitch and a larger opening; a narrower shape causes a higher pitch and a smaller opening. The central part of the shape (the belly), or the point of noticeable taper, forms a fulcrum which is the point over which a leverage principle is used when the cane is bound on the staple (Illust. 58a and b). For example, the more wood put on the staple (spreading the cane apart at that end), the smaller the opening becomes across the fulcrum; the less wood put on the staple, the larger the opening will be. As a result of this, the spot where the widest point of the shape (the fulcrum) falls in relation to the tip and throat is important. The width of the throat usually affects the distance that the cane must be bound on the staple.

When coupled with a particular gouge measurement, staple, instrument, and embouchure, the shape of the reed becomes an important link in the chain of sound-producing equipment. A recent worldwide survey of artist reeds shows a width variation of from 6.10 mm. to 8.00 mm. Some of these reeds were noticeably modified from the original shaper by shaving the sides of the reed with a knife.

The shape and the gouge are two important elements that determine how much the distribution and quantity of the wood must be modified later on by the cutting process. Shaper blades of different dimensions are shown in Illust. 34. The three critical parts (top, center, and throat) can be compared by using the lines which extend across the page.

Some oboists will use more than one shaper. For the beginner who has no basis for judgment, a medium dimension shape (Illust 34b) is a good choice. A usable width at the widest point of the reed is 7 mm., even though most reeds are slightly narrower than this. A fairly full throat rather than a small one is desirable.

It is a mistake to recommend a definite measurement to an experienced performer. He may decide that he likes best the one he started out with, but in the meantime he will have tried others.

Commercial cane is available gouged, gouged and shaped, or gouged, shaped, and folded. Shapers are available in which several pieces of cane can be shaped at once. These do not require the cane to be folded as do most conventional shapers. Therefore, the term *folded* should be used when ordering to be sure that the cane is folded. The novice should purchase a shaper of his own and start using gouged or straight cane only after learning some of the basic principles of the cutting process.

The first step in the shaping process is soaking the cane. Cane of different degrees of porosity will take up water in varying lengths of time. About forty-five minutes to one hour in room-temperature water (or until the cane sinks) is sufficient soaking time for most gouged cane. Sometimes air bubbles that are gathered on the cane must be dislodged so the cane can sink in a reasonable length of time. Some reedmakers advocate boiling the cane. There are differences of opinion as to the soaking time for cane that is to be shaped as well as cane that is to be gouged. There is agreement on one thing, however; the cane must not be soaked too long.

Next, the cane is placed on the easel and both ends are tapered, starting about 4 mm. up on the cane, allowing the cane to be bound smoothly on the staple (Illust. 35). A difference in playing quality may occur if these ends are not tapered. In the above-mentioned world survey of reeds, it was found that 98 per cent of them were tapered and bound smoothly on the staple.

Next, the cane is marked at the center line of the easel by rolling the knife blade over the rind

(text continued on p. 71) **63**

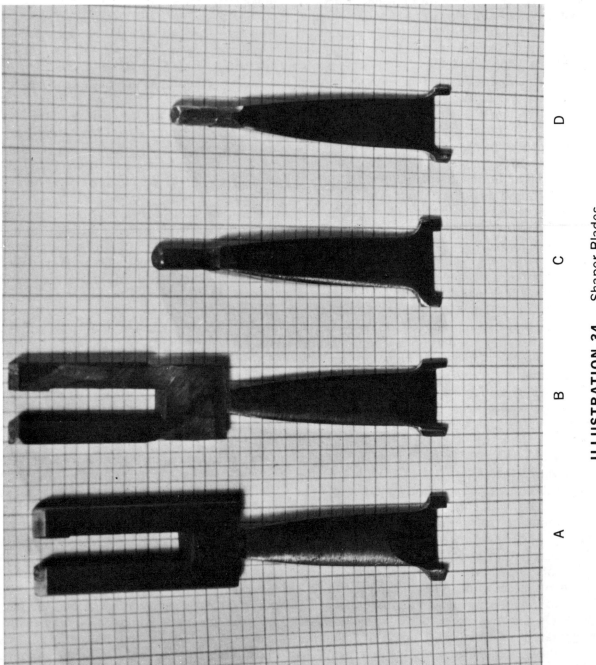

A   B   C   D

ILLUSTRATION 34   Shaper Blades

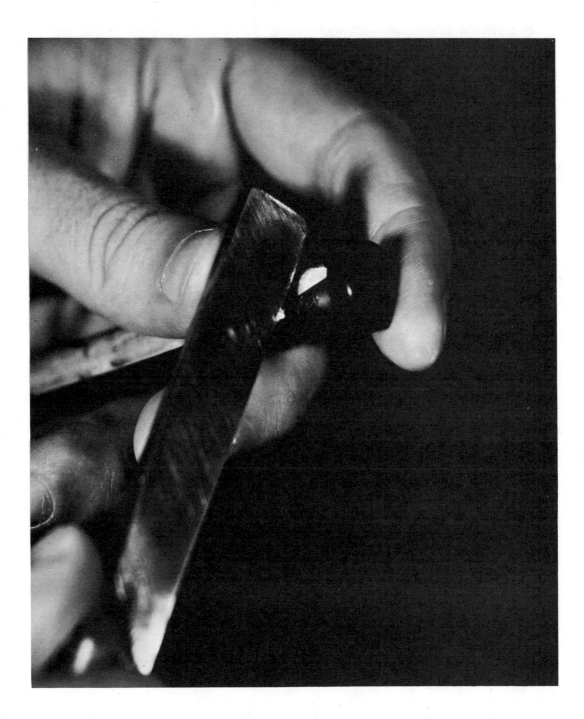

ILLUSTRATION 35   Trimming the Cane ends

ILLUSTRATION 36   Marking the center line

66

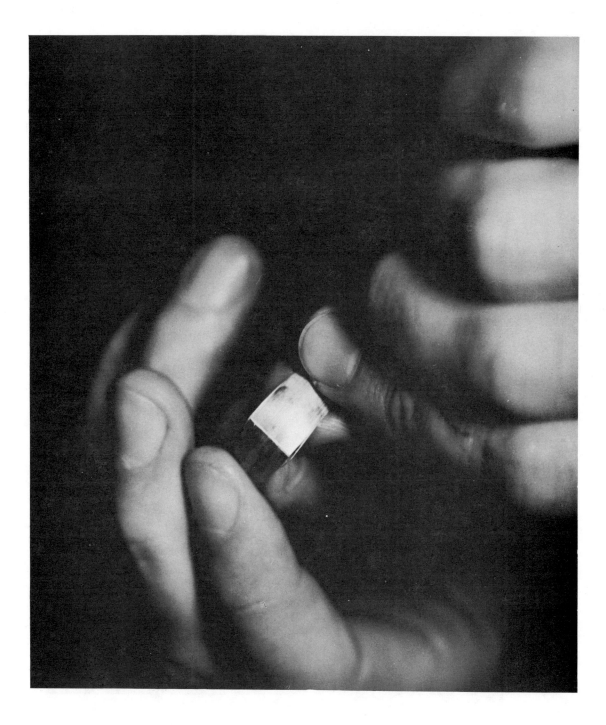

ILLUSTRATION 37   Folding the Cane

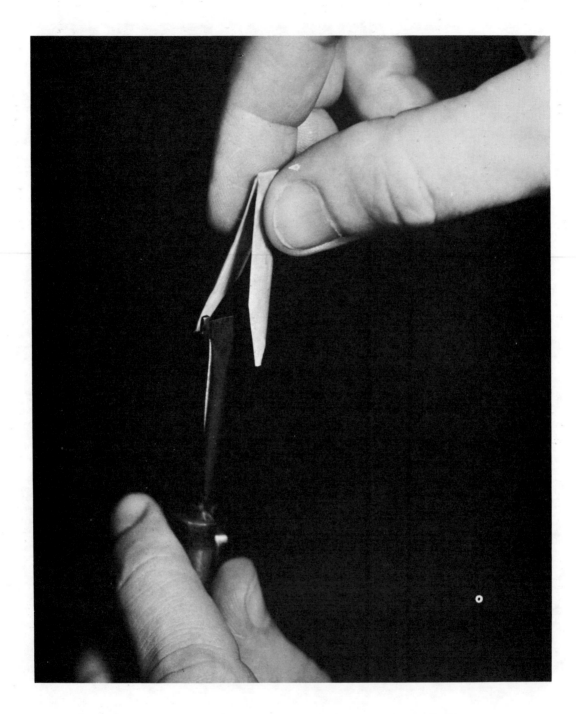

ILLUSTRATION 38   Placing Cane on the Shaper

ILLUSTRATION 39   Shaping the Cane

ILLUSTRATION 40   Shaping completed

about three times, using medium light downward pressure (Illust. 36). The cut is not made so deeply that the cane breaks completely through nor so lightly that it splits when folded.

The cane is then removed from the easel and folded (Illust. 37). After marking, the cane can also be folded by bending it over a knife blade. The cane is then placed on the shaper blade (Illust. 38). If the cane is too wide for the top of the shaper it is trimmed equally on both sides at the fold. After adjusting the grain of the cane to run exactly up and down the blade, the holders which secure the cane to the shaper are tightened at the bottom. The center of the gouge should run up and down the center of the blade. An equal amount of cane will usually show on either side of the blade.

The cane is then shaped to the blade by draw-ing a knife blade down the sides (Illust. 39). The blade should be kept even across the sides of the shaper or the results will be uneven. Another good shaping tool is a razor blade set in a paint scraper handle that adjusts to a 90° angle. The razor blade sharpens easily on a stone; this saves the edges of your better knives. Caution should be used to shape both sides as evenly as possible so that they match. The four sides of the shaped cane will measure the same at any given point opposite each other if the gouge is even.

Illust. 40 shows a piece of cane after it has been shaped. Some reedmakers remove the cane from the shaper and allow it to dry before binding on the staple; others bind while it is still wet from shaping.

The Binding Process

There is little variation in the binding operation in comparison to the other processes. Most reedmakers agree that binding should start one to five turns from the end of the staple. The reed is then bound up to the end of the staple, the binding crosses over, and then terminates at, or close to, the cork. Binding is not done past the end of the staple. Sometimes beeswax is used on the thread before binding. Most reedmakers now use nylon for binding instead of silk, with red the predominant color. Some reedmakers coat the complete binding with a preparation such as fingernail polish.

First, about two feet of nylon is unwound from the spool and passed over beeswax about three times, holding it into the beeswax with the left thumb while the beeswax is held in the left hand. Excessive wax will moisten the nylon too much, causing it to break under tension. The wax seals any possible cracks between individual turns of the binding.

The end of the nylon is tied to a hook that will stand fairly strenuous tension. The back upright of a chair can be used. Do not use a good piece of dining room furniture for this purpose because the nylon will mark the wood. Use either a metal folding chair or any straight-backed wooden chair suitable for this purpose. Other useful nylon holders are water faucets, doorknobs, automobile door handles, trunk handles, etc. Another method of securing the loose end of the nylon is to wad paper into a tight ball about six inches in diameter; tie or wrap the nylon around this ball, place the ball between the knees, and pull against it.

Rewind about half the nylon back on the spool after the end is tied. A spool, cork, or dowel can serve as a holder. Caution must be used, however, because under adequate tension the nylon, if held in the bare hand, will cut the skin.

Next, place the piece of shaped cane on a staple (Illust. 41). The distance approximately halfway to the cork (7 or 8 mm.) should be correct for a test. Right-handed people should hold the staple in the left hand and the cane in the right. The straight line represented by the fold of the tip of the cane should be exactly across the long measurement of the elliptical end of the staple.

Many oboists insert the mandrel into the staple before starting to bind. Theoretically, the flat side of the handle of the mandrel should be in line with the wide measurement of the elliptical end of the staple. Therefore, the straight fold of the cane should be lined up with the flat part of the handle on the assumption it will then be in line with the elliptical opening; however, some mandrels are not in line with themselves, or have round handles which makes this impossible.

The writer has in the past inserted the mandrel before taking a turn with the nylon, but now prefers to insert the mandrel after a turn or two has been taken around the cane because one can then look through the staple to see if the cane is

(text continued on p. 80)

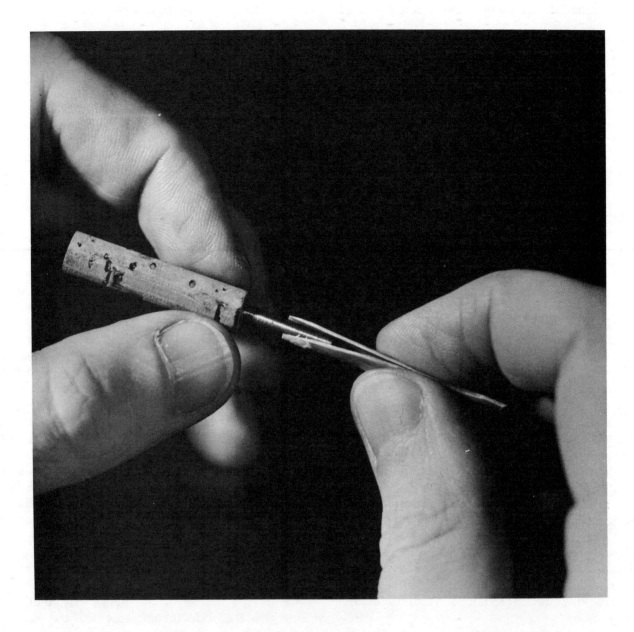

ILLUSTRATION 41   Placing Cane on Staple

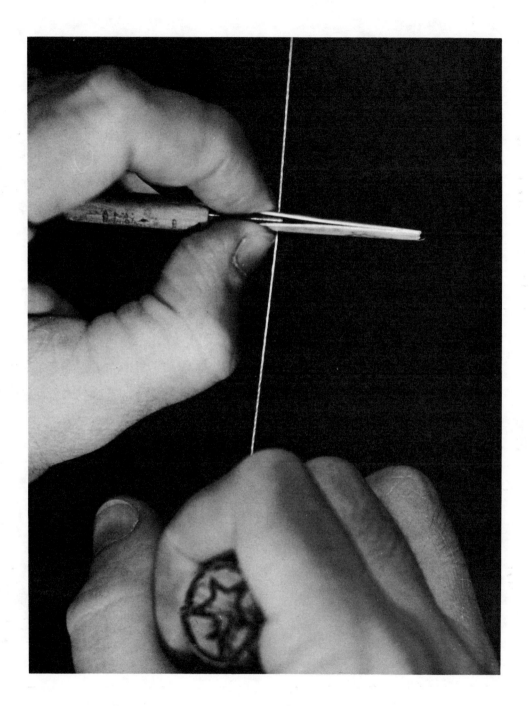

ILLUSTRATION 42   Correct position for Nylon

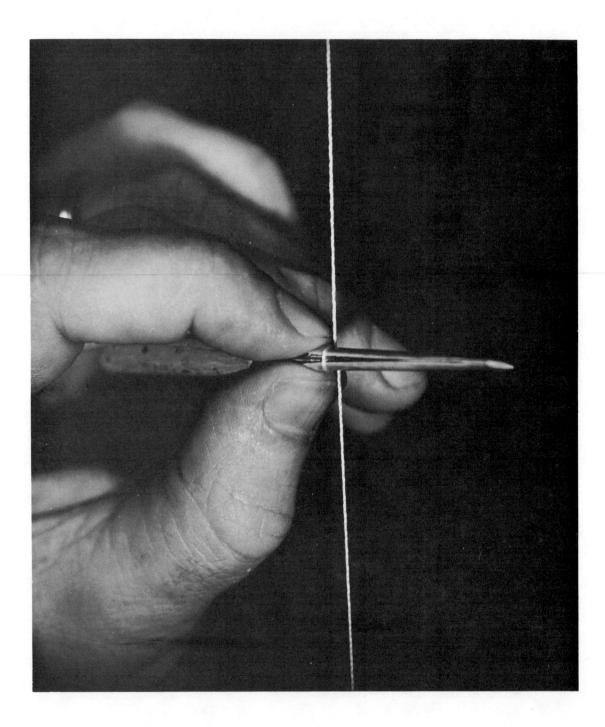

ILLUSTRATION 43   One turn around Cane

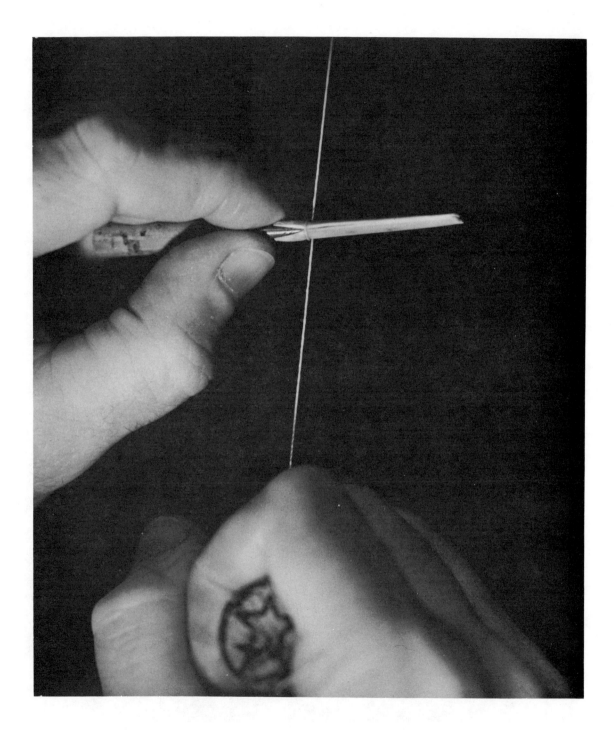

ILLUSTRATION 44   Cane pulled tight

ILLUSTRATION 45   Two turns pulled tight

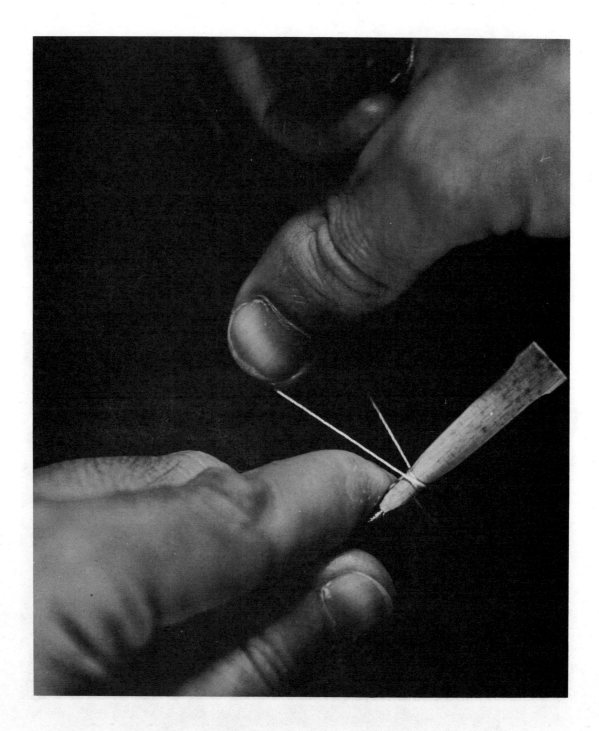

ILLUSTRATION 46   Crossing over

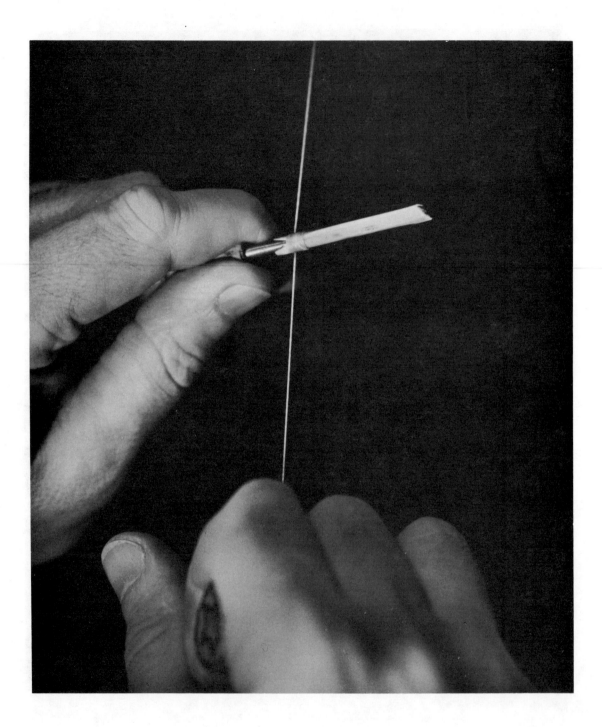

ILLUSTRATION 47   Winding toward the Cork

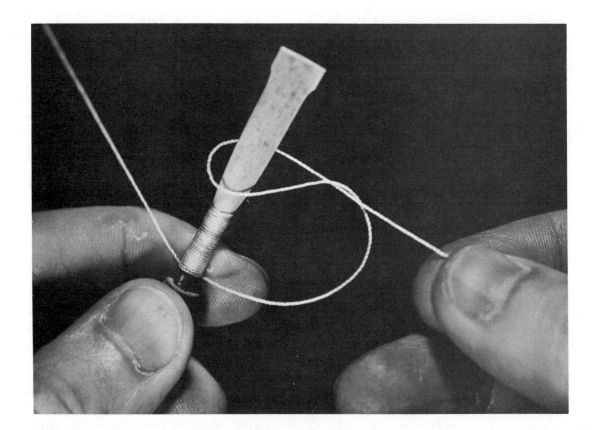

ILLUSTRATION 48　　　　　　Making a half-hitch

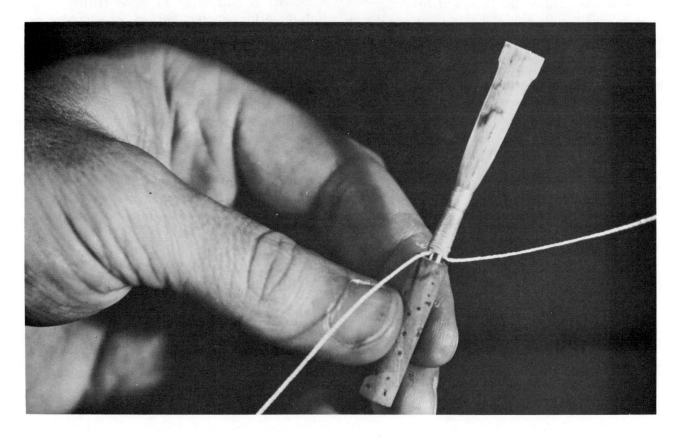

ILLUSTRATION 49　　　　　　Completed binding

lined up correctly. Inserting the mandrel later would benefit those reedmakers who have mandrels with round handles. The mandrel keeps the staple from being squeezed out of shape from the tension of the nylon. Consequently, it should be inserted as soon as possible after the proper alignment is ascertained.

The cane should be lined up lengthwise with the staple, not tilted to the right or left, back or front. The tension applied by the nylon can pull the cane out of alignment if the staple is not scored several times. These score marks bite into the cane and help hold it in position while the binding is taking place.

Next the cane is held as shown in Illust. 42 and is placed on the nylon about eight inches from the hook or chair where it is tied; the winding begins about two turns from the end of the staple. The writer prefers to start at this point rather than four or five turns below the end of the staple because it is easier to slacken tension and adjust if the sides of the cane are not meeting properly.

A turn around the cane is then made (Illust. 43) and pulled tight (Illust. 44). Both sides are checked to see if they are meeting equally. If they are not, tension is slackened while the cane is pushed with either the thumb or forefinger of the left hand to the side that has the most opening. If the sides will not close one turn before the end of the staple is reached, tension on the nylon should be released and about 1 mm. more cane pushed on the staple. The nylon can then be tightened again. If necessary, the cane can be adjusted to one side or the other so the two sides will meet simultaneously. If the sides close too soon, tension should be slackened while the cane is pulled about 1 mm. off the staple and tightened again.

Both sides of the cane should meet equally one turn before the binding reaches the end of the staple (Illust. 44). The final turn should close the sides without squeezing them any tighter than necessary to prevent air from leaking out. One should never bind past the end of the staple.

Cane which is shaped on the same shaper should close at nearly the same place every time. The shape and sometimes the dimension (oval and taper) of the staple govern the amount of cane to be placed on it. The beginner may have to test several times before getting the cane to close properly at the right spot. After some practice in the manipulation of cane, the process becomes easier. For the beginner, binding is largely a problem of knowing what to do with his hands.

Two turns on the cane are shown in Illust. 45. The mandrel should be inserted at this point after looking through the staple to check that the flat of the cane runs parallel to the elliptical end of the staple. When the sides meet as prescribed above, the thread is crossed over (Illust. 46) and winding is begun toward the cork. The tension should be constantly maintained, as each turn is bound tightly against the preceding one (Illust. 47).

When about 3 mm. from the cork, the nylon is held with the left index finger to keep it from slipping. A half-hitch is made (Illust. 48), slid into position at the bottom of the binding and pulled tight. One or two more tight half-hitches are made and the nylon cut off close to the last knot. A spot of cement is then dropped on the knot to keep it from coming loose. A bound and tied reed is shown in Illust. 49.

The mandrel is removed to check the alignment of the reed; if it is not straight, it should be bound over again. To get a piece of cane off the staple, the cross-over strand at the top of the binding should be cut. The binding will then unwind easily all the way to the bottom, especially if it is under fairly heavy tension.

The Scraping Process

The process of scraping a reed so it will play well is not as difficult as it may seem. A few basic concepts will simplify the subject.

1. The scraped portion of the cane is divided into three areas:

    a. *The tip* is the very tip, approximately 1/4 to 1/2 mm. long.

    b. *The lay* is the tapered section from the tip to where the back begins; this area usually contains the *heart*.

    c. *The back* begins at the thickest point of the lay and includes the rest of the area that is scraped (sometimes almost down to the binding).

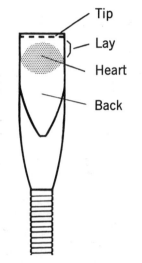

ILLUSTRATION 50   Areas of a reed

2. The cutting or scraping process consists of taking wood off the tip, lay, and back of the reed blank so the cane will vibrate in the desired way. Any one of the three basic areas can be varied in length and thickness to balance the other two areas. Adjustment is necessary if one of the areas is unbalanced with either of the others.

3. The word *scrape* denotes the total areas of tip, lay, and back. It is analogous to the style or type of reed.

4. The characteristics of a good reed are:

    a. correct pitch
    b. correct resistance
    c. adequate opening
    d. adequate dynamic range
    e. tonal quality

These are discussed in detail in the following chapter.

5. Beginning reedmakers lack guideposts or perspective from which to judge the various stages of the scraping process. The following concept should help clarify the process. *The tip and lay are finished as nearly as possible; wood is then taken off the back to balance the other two areas.* The stages between are merely means to insure that the above is completed efficiently. After the reed reaches the playing stage, the remainder of the scraping process becomes a matter of adjustment.

The reed blank is first soaked for about fifteen minutes in a small glass of water, with the water level almost up to the binding of the reed.

Illust. 51. The water is then removed and the reed is measured to find where the eventual tip should be placed. A good length to start with is 70 mm. If the reeds require a different length in order to have a better pitch level, the measurements should be altered accordingly.

Illust. 52a. The sides of the cane are marked about 4 mm. down from the eventual tip. All four marks should be opposite each other and the marking done at an angle.

Illust. 52b. A half-moon shape is completed in the bark. Both sides of the blank should be as nearly identical as possible.

Illust. 52c. The bark remaining from the half-moon out to the tip is removed.

Illust. 52d. The tip is thinned and cut open; then the plaque is inserted. Illust. 54 and 55 show a method of inserting the plaque without endangering the tip of the reed.

Illust. 53a. The cane is thinned out (always scraping outward from the center in a half-moon contour) to shape the lay and tip.

Illust. 53b. The formation of the lay and tip is continued, then trimmed almost to length. The trimming of the tip on the cutting block is shown in Illust. 56.

Illust. 53c. When the tip and lay are finished as much as they can be at this stage, the bark is taken off the back from the lay toward the binding. The bark is taken off out to the edges, but little, if any, is removed from the edges themselves.

Illust. 53d. The tip is thinned again. If necessary, the lay is smoothed without touching the heart to any great extent. More bark is then cut off the back.

At this point, the reed should "crow" fairly well. It should also play when put on the oboe. Of course, how well it plays depends upon the amount and proportion of wood that has been taken off the tip, lay, and back. In this regard, please see Illustrations 53d, 57f, 63 and 64. These are examples of reeds cut by three oboists. It should be noted again that there are many styles of reedmaking and those reeds shown in Illustrations 53d, 57f and 64 are offered as examples of a well-defined American style.

Little mention has been made of the heart of the reed. Some wood must be cut from this area in order to balance it with the other areas. Care should be taken not to take off too much wood from the heart. It is simple to take wood off, but impossible to put it back!

Illust. 57f. The tips have been thinned and trimmed. More wood is taken from the lay and hump and considerably more from the back. Illust. 57f shows an interesting result of reed adjustments. Both reeds are close to the same pitch level of A = 440 despite their obvious differences of length. The reed on the right is slightly sharper because of the shorter lay and short length, but the high pitch has been compensated for by taking more wood from the back. The reed on the left is slightly more flat in pitch because of the longer lay and more length. Consequently, less wood has been removed from the back. These visual differences in adjustment are due in large part to unequal texture and/or gouge of the individual pieces of cane.

Here are a few general hints on the adjustment of some common reed faults after the reed has been brought to the playing stage:

1. *Reed too hard to blow.* The tip should be thin. Wood should be taken lightly from lay, sides of lay, hump, and back. The reed should be tried often during this process.

2. *Reed too easy to blow.* Too much wood has been removed. The reed should be cut off at the tip, the tip thinned, and the lay and back remade accordingly.

3. *Low notes unresponsive.* This is usually caused by too much resistance. Wood should be taken from the sides of the lay where it nearly meets the back. Resistance should then be adjusted in the hump, back, or heart if necessary.

4. *High notes flat.* The tip should be trimmed and the opening made smaller with adjustments for less resistance.

5. *Pitch level of the reed is high and quality is shallow.* The scrape should be lengthened by removing a small amount of wood from the back or

sides of the lay. The tip, lay, or back should be made longer.

6. *Pitch level of the reed is low.* The shape should be narrowed if the pitch is just slightly flat. The tip is trimmed, while the lay and back are balanced accordingly until the desired pitch level is achieved.

7. *Crow too high-pitched and shrill.* This usually means that the tip, lay, or back is too short. In other words, not enough wood has been removed from some area(s). Wood should be removed proportionately from the tip, lay, and back. Sometimes, dependent upon the placement of the crow, it is better to take wood only from the back or off the hump.

8. *Crow too low, soft, or woozy.* The scrape is usually too long; that is, too much wood has been removed from some area(s). The tip should be trimmed and thinned, then the reed should be tried on the oboe. If the pitch level is flat, the tip should be trimmed and the lay and back rescraped accordingly.

Following are a few pointers which have been passed over until now so that the scraping process could be kept to a reasonably concise outline.

1. A goose-necked lamp with a 60-watt bulb is an excellent work light.

2. The cane should be kept moist enough throughout the scraping process to prevent it from splitting.

3. The cane should not be pushed down hard on the plaque, as the tip will split easily under pressure. A sharp knife must always be used.

4. In its finished state, the tip should be thin. Sometimes a tip can be thinned better during a period of several days when the cane is dry.

5. It is sometimes helpful to remove the plaque during the scraping process, and hold the reed up in front of the light. This back-lighting will show the contour and the thickness of the cane. Probably the most graphic way to see what has been done with the scrape is to top-light the reed (hold the reed so that the light from the desk lamp shines down its length). If held at the correct angle, the hills and valleys of the scrape will be thrown into sharp relief. Top-lighting is illustrated in Illustrations 52, 53, and 57.

6. The crow is usually an indication of how the reed will play when placed in the oboe. The crow is the high-pitched rattle emitted by a reed when it is placed too far in the mouth (almost to the binding) and blown. The correct pitch for the crow is approximately third-space C in the treble staff. Some good reeds do not crow; nevertheless,

(text continued on p. 89)

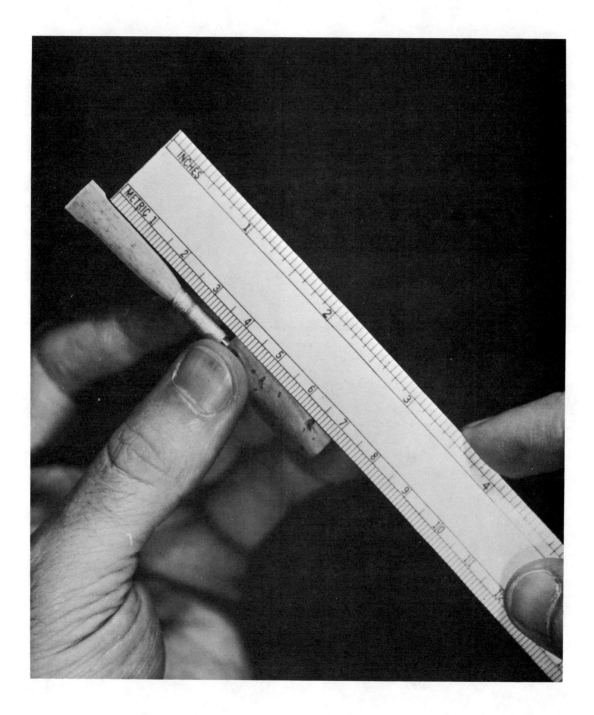

ILLUSTRATION 51   Measuring the length

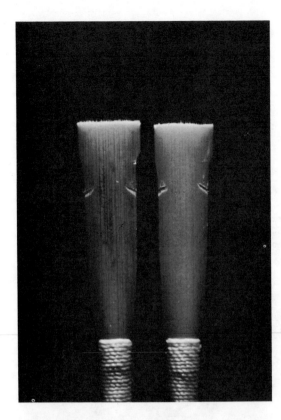

A. First Stage

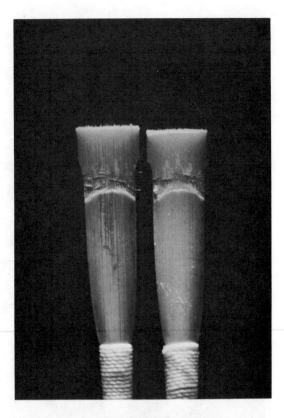

B. Second Stage

C. Third Stage

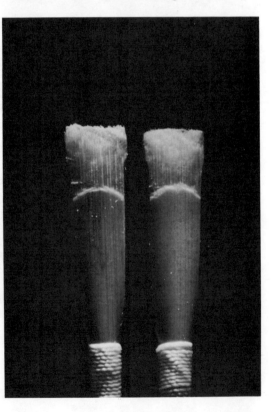

D. Fourth Stage

ILLUSTRATION 52

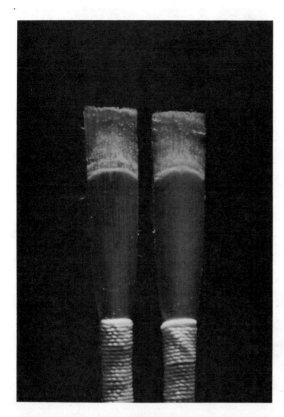

A. Fifth Stage

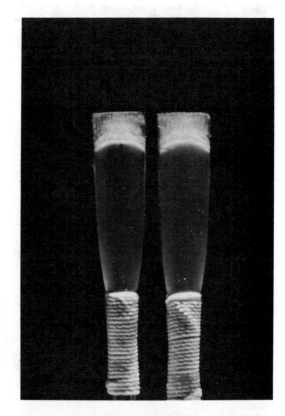

B. Sixth Stage

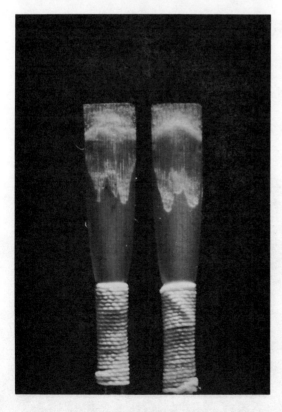

C. Seventh Stage

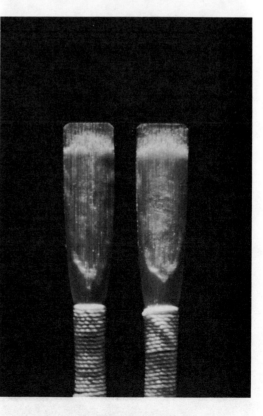

D. Eighth Stage

ILLUSTRATION 53

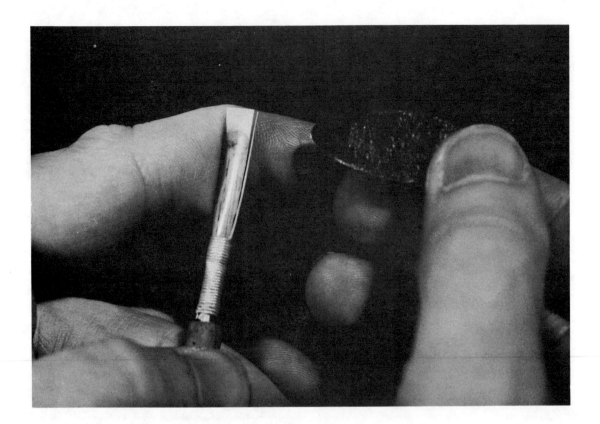

ILLUSTRATION 54

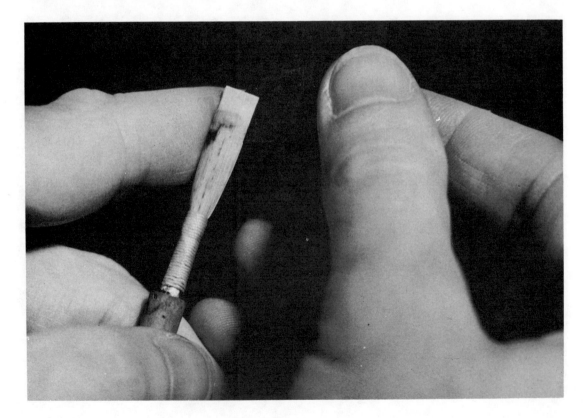

ILLUSTRATION 55   Inserting the Plaque

ILLUSTRATION 56   Trimming the tip

A. First Stage

B. Second Stage

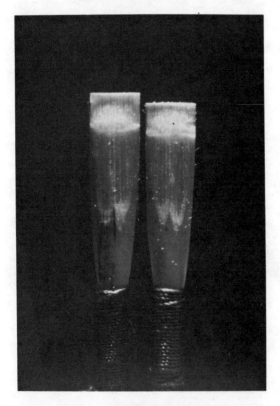

C. Third Stage

D. Fourth Stage

ILLUSTRATION 57

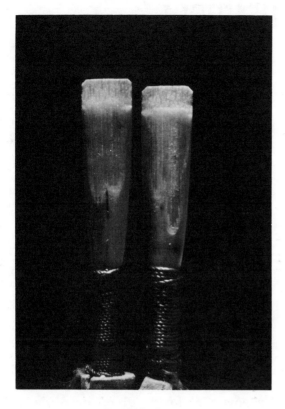

E. Fifth Stage

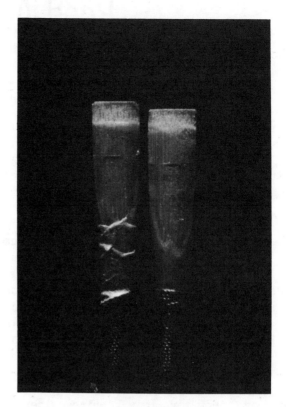

F. Sixth Stage

ILLUSTRATION 57

a crow is useful in adjusting the reed.

7. The drying process of a reed is dependent upon the humidity in the air, air circulation around the reed, porosity of the cane, temperature, etc. A reed kept in a reed case will not dry as fast as one left in the open air. The warming, drying influence of the work lamp is conducive to drying. Generally, overnight or a twenty-four hour period is sufficient time. Soaking swells the fibers and grain of the cane; drying shrinks the fibers. This is especially noticeable in soft-textured, young, green cane. Hard-textured cane reacts less to soaking. Cane will react much as a piece of lumber does if soaked with water and allowed to dry in the sun; the grain of the wood will raise. This change is less noticeable in well-seasoned lumber or cane. The raised grain can be scraped off and the soaking repeated. After several repetitions the cane ceases to "pick up wood" and becomes more stable. This is an important factor in reed-making because any adding or subtracting, swelling or contracting of fibers will affect the playing characteristics of the reed. This change takes place mostly during drying-out periods.

After some experience is gained, the reed-maker may wish to compress or expand the preliminary stages of the scraping process. For example, it is a good practice to start taking bark from the back before the tip and lay are complete. This releases the tension in the back which tends to hold the opening too wide. As has been noted, pressing a wide opening against a plaque may split the reed. Another example of elision is making the lay immediately after carving the half-moon in the bark. Many reed-makers start from the blank piece of cane and immediately begin the tip and lay. They have made so many reeds that they have developed a good eye for proportion and a "feel" for the cane.

Many experienced reedmakers work on the tip, lay, and back all at the same time. This is difficult for the beginner because it involves balancing three different areas against the other two. Balancing several areas at once may be simple for the experienced reedmaker because he has developed his method over the years, but for the beginner, this method is complex and usually ends in confusion.

Reed Adjustment

This chapter is concerned with the scraping of the reed after it has reached the stage where it will crow and will produce a sound on the oboe. Essentially, adjustment is based upon musical demand, aural concept, and physical necessity. This implies balancing the component factors, or basic areas of the reed, to suit the reedmaker.

Musical Demand

Some music requires the use of extreme ranges; high, low, or both. Second oboists usually have different technical problems than first oboists since a lower range is imposed upon them by the music. The performer may prefer a slightly different tonal quality for a particular piece of music. For example, a composition by Bach may require a different sound than Debussy. Some pieces may be predominantly *legato;* some may require a great deal of *staccato* playing. Compositions or conductors may require extremes of *pp* or *ff*. Usually the oboist tries to make a reed that will meet *all* the demands of the music, but he is not always successful. The pitch level, ease of articulation, dynamic range, quality, and ease in the production of over-all range of notes are seldom perfect, but they are usually adequate.

Aural Concept

Most professional oboists have a definite idea as to what their tonal quality should be. These preferences have given rise to several schools of reedmaking. Although the embouchure, instrument, and room acoustics are important factors, the reed itself is one of the most important members of the sound-producing team because tonal quality can be altered so easily by its adjustment. Beginners should take every opportunity to hear good oboists, both on records and in person, so that they may develop as soon as possible an aural concept of the oboe's sound.

Physical Necessity

Physical necessity refers mainly to the individual aspects of the oboist's embouchure and breath capacity. No two embouchures are exactly alike, but they are similar enough to have certain common characteristics. They control the reed opening, keep the air from leaking out of the mouth, and more or less cover the lay of the reed. The latitude in these three processes de- pends upon the individual embouchure. An oboist may prefer a slightly more open or closed reed aperture because of his embouchure. Breath capacity and breathing habits are somewhat different among individual players; therefore, the oboist may require a reed that blows with more or less resistance in order to meet his own peculiarities. These variable factors, the opening and the resistance, can be balanced along with other important characteristics while the reed is being adjusted.

The following paragraphs list and discuss the usual factors which affect the five basic characteristics of a good reed. If the reedmaker wishes to adjust a reed, he does so by varying one or more of these factors.

The most important factor is probably the *diameter of the tube cane* from which the piece of cane was cut. Because the final reed opening is proportional to the diameter of the cane, a reed made from a tube that is too large in diameter will have a smaller opening because the natural arch of the cane is not great enough to hold open the aperture of the reed. A reed cut from a tube that is too small in diameter will tend to have too great an opening because the natural arch of the cane holds the aperture of the reed too far open. Depending upon the climate, hard-textured cane usually demands a larger diameter tube than softer cane in order to give the finished reed a usable aperture.

The amount of wood removed proportionately from the tip, lay, and back of the reed will affect the opening somewhat, but very little. Too much wood should not be removed just to make the opening smaller. The arch of the cane is the most important factor.

Adjustment of the opening can be accomplished by *moving the cane on or off the staple*. Placing the cane farther on the staple will make the tip opening smaller. This is caused by a fulcrum which is formed approximately in the area where the shape begins to taper noticeably when the binding is applied, and brings a lever principle into play. When one end is made larger, the other becomes smaller, and vice versa (Illust. 58a and b).

Adjustment of the opening is theoretically possible by *changing the dimension of the staple*. A longer staple would have a more gradual taper.

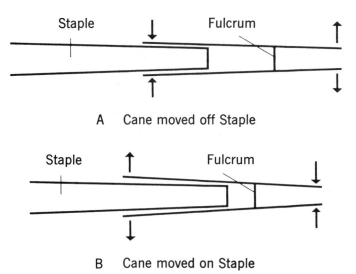

A   Cane moved off Staple

B   Cane moved on Staple

ILLUSTRATION 58

Thus, a slightly larger opening in the reed could be expected. A shorter staple would give the opposite result. However, the difference in the opening of the reed between a 46 mm. and 48 mm. staple would be so slight that it might be overpowered by the arch and gouge of the cane and the scrape of the reed.

A better method of adjusting the opening by changing the dimension of the staple can be effected by inserting the mandrel in the staple and applying pressure with pliers at the points illustrated. Illust. 59 and 60 show how to make the opening *larger*; Illust. 61 and 62 how to make the opening *smaller*. It is helpful to make this adjustment when the reed is at the illustrated stage of development, especially if the opening is too large. The writer has found that openings must be closed much more often than opened.

Adjustable factors affecting the *pitch* of a reed are:

The over-all length should be shortened (to make the pitch *higher*) by trimming the required amount from the tip, thus shortening the amount of cane showing above the binding. Some oboists cut off the bottom of the staple. The writer has had unhappy results with this procedure because cutting off the bottom end of the staple changed the proportion of the staple in relation to the bore of his particular oboe. The bottom diameter of the staple becomes slightly smaller when cut off, tending to make the upper register play flat. Sometimes it encourages "gurgling" on the low notes and makes the middle register (B, C, and C♯) more out of tune. If a shorter staple length is required, the writer prefers to purchase a custom-made staple of the desired length so that the bottom and top diameter dimensions can still

be correct. It is obvious that wood or pieces of staple that have already been cut off cannot be put back. Therefore, if the pitch is too high, the reedmaker should not have cut the staple or cut the tip of the reed to begin with.

The *width of the shape* may be adjusted to change the pitch. A wide shape will cause a *lower* pitch; a narrow shape, a *higher* pitch. The common adjustment is to narrow the shape carefully by shaving the sides of the reed slightly with the knife.

The *size of the opening* will affect the pitch. The opening can be adjusted as noted earlier in this chapter. An opening made smaller will usually *raise* the pitch; made larger, will usually *lower* the pitch.

Daniel McAninch, in a doctoral thesis at the Eastman School of Music, states that "attacks of high notes are often uncertain as to pitch and tone quality. If the player uses a reed with a large or fairly large opening, he will have to employ a great deal of lip pressure to obtain the high tones. Also, the pitch of the high tones will be regulated considerably by the amount of lip pressure used. A reed with a long tip will also handicap the performer in obtaining the high tones. A long tip on a reed tends to flatten the pitch of the whole reed, but particularly in the upper register. A shorter tip will make the upper register sharper in pitch in relation to the middle register and will facilitate the production of the extreme high notes."

A tight *embouchure* will close the opening and, therefore, *raise* the pitch. Playing with too much reed in the mouth will also tend to close the opening and raise the pitch. It is better to play fairly far out on the tip of the reed and stabilize the pitch by adopting a different over-all length of reed. The reed length should be planned to play A=440 when the staple is pushed all the way to the bottom of the tenon.

Oboes have different pitch levels. If the pitch level of the instrument is unreasonably sharp or flat, enough so that adjustment of the reed cannot correct the over-all level, another instrument should be used.

The amount of wood removed proportionately from the back, lay, and tip of the reed will affect the pitch. Generally, the more wood removed from the back, the *lower* the pitch. A longer lay will tend to *lower* the pitch. A long tip will sometimes result in a *lower* pitch.

Resistance. The amount of resistance to breath or embouchure in the reed can be lessened by *removing wood* from the tip, lay, or back of the reed. Wood may be scraped off individual areas (the tip, lay, or back, sides of lay, heart, or hump) to reduce resistance within that area or from several areas at once. However, if wood is scraped from one area, the others, by comparison, are left thicker. This is a valuable concept when one wishes to "add" more wood to a particular spot. For example, by thinning the tip, the heart becomes thicker. The guide for adjusting resistance in a new reed is the tip. If the tip is as thin as possible, the lay, heart, and back can be balanced to it more easily because the tip is then a definite, unchangeable factor, and one variable has been removed. If the tip is not as thin as possible, the other areas will be proportionately thicker, and consequently the reed will have too much resistance. Also, if the tip is not thin and the other two areas are thinned out, the two areas will be out of balance with the thick tip; thus, tonal quality and response will suffer.

Response is another aspect of resistance. It is usually true that a reed with little resistance will have an easy response. But a reed with too little resistance is as undesirable as one with too much. Too much resistance in a reed can place insurmountable difficulties in the path of the embouchure, response, articulation (tongue), intonation, vibrato, endurance, and efficiently relaxed playing. The resistance norm to be desired is the one in which the player can operate at the greatest possible efficiency. This norm varies greatly among oboists. The response may be adjusted by taking wood from the following areas: the tip, *the sides of the lay*, the heart, the hump, and the back. At times, a reed will seem stuffy and will not respond well because the binding has squeezed the sides of the cane together at the top of the staple. This can sometimes be freed by running a plaque down to the binding between the sides of the reed. If this does not help the response, the reed should be rebound.

Another factor which affects resistance and response is the *gouge* of the cane. Generally, a thicker gouge will tend to be more resistant and less responsive than a thinner gouge. However, if the gouge dimension is within reason, this can be balanced by cutting more wood off the reed.

Dynamic Range. Probably the most important variable factor that affects the dynamic range of a reed is the *opening*. A larger opening gives greater volume; a smaller opening gives less volume. When a reed is played upon, the opening can only be made *smaller*, because it is almost impossible to open it with the embouchure or

with breath pressure. If the opening is small to begin with and the oboist relaxes the embouchure to allow the reed to open and get more volume, the reed cannot open further, and there will be no more volume. If the reed is *too* open, the player's embouchure will be working to hold the opening down to a normal level, instead of being able to relax. This makes a *pp* doubly difficult because the embouchure must almost completely close the reed for such a low volume level.

The logical solution is to play on an opening that will give the greatest amount of flexibility in dynamic range, etc. Start with an opening that can reasonably be controlled by the embouchure.

Openings, aside from the dimension and shape of the aperture, can also be flexible or inflexible depending upon the texture of the cane and the amount of wood removed (principally from the tip and lay). Flexible tips are sometimes referred to as "springy" tips.

Cane texture is another factor which affects dynamic range. Nearly all oboists have had reeds made from porous, soggy cane that seemed choked and had only a *pp* to *mf* volume range regardless of the opening. Not much can be done about this. Uusually, if one cuts on a piece of cane of this nature to free the sound, he will have to scrape so much that the reed will become too easy blowing.

Tonal Quality is the result of the number, distribution, and relative intensities of overtones that are present in a tone. Bell Telephone Laboratories have issued a limited edition of important recordings which aurally illustrate this fact. Tones from several instruments are played a number of times, and each time overtones are added or subtracted by an electronic filter. By selectively filtering the overtones in this manner, a tone can either be broken down from a rich to a pure tone or can be built up from a pure tone to a rich one. By progressively adding the necessary overtones along with their relative distribution and intensity, a sound can be built up to acquire a particular character. A discussion of the overtone series is not necessary in this text. Several excellent articles on the subject are available in the standard books on acoustics.

Theoretically, if the oboist could set up a chart (depending upon his subjective judgment of quality) of the desirable overtone patterns and pitch standards for a representative range of his instrument, he could, by adjusting his reeds, arrive at more closely controlled results. Each tone on the instrument will have a slightly different overtone pattern, but there will be enough

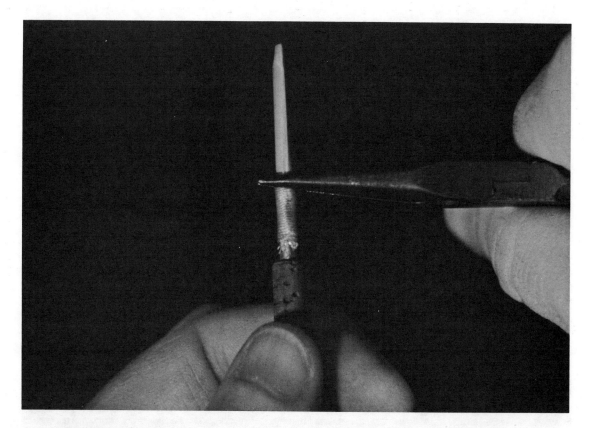

ILLUSTRATION 59

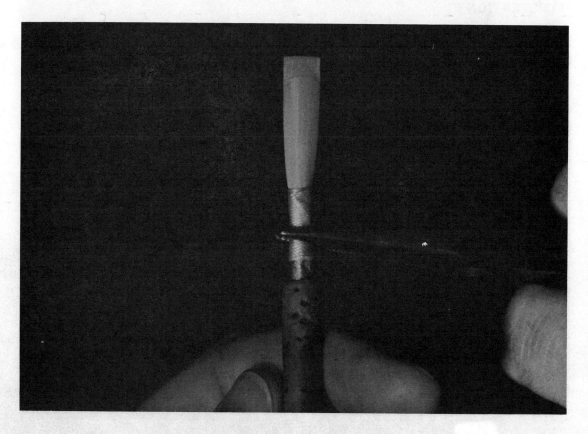

ILLUSTRATION 60   Enlarging the Reed opening
(Insert mandrel in staple)

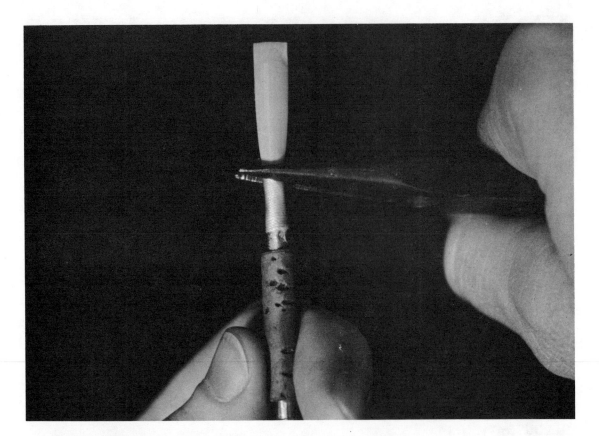

ILLUSTRATION 61

ILLUSTRATION 62

Closing the Reed opening
(Insert mandrel in staple)

similarity in the patterns so that the sound should remain characteristic.

If pitch, resistance, and dynamic range are well balanced, the tonal quality of a reed is usually acceptable. The effect of the embouchure and the acoustical properties of the individual oboe are important agents in the final sound; however, this discussion is primarily concerned with the place of the reed in the chain of sound-producing equipment.

The reed vibrates entirely and in parts so as to produce a certain composite of fundamental and overtones. Adjusting the tonal quality of a reed involves changing the vibration pattern of this fundamental and these overtones to a pattern that is more desirable.

Two useful concepts for adjusting the reed quality are:

1. Predominance of tip vibration causes a *brighter* quality because the vibrations are short and therefore facilitate the production of high overtones.

2. Predominance of back vibration causes a *darker* quality because the vibrations are long and therefore facilitate the production of low overtones.

These concepts can also be charted in the following manner:

    tip   = short vibrations = high pitch or
            overtones
    back = long vibrations = low pitch or
            overtones
    lay   = heart or core of the sound

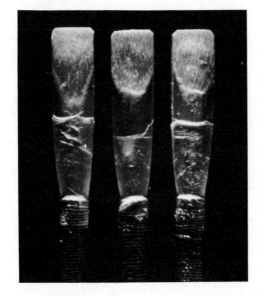

ILLUSTRATION 63

To illustrate, the traditional French scrape can be compared with the scrape in Illustration 63. These are the reeds of Mr. Raymond Claro of the Opéra Comique. The French scrape has a rather long tip and the back is left relatively untouched. The back does not vibrate much because it is still covered with bark; consequently, many of the long vibrations in the timbre are absent. The sound is bright because there is a comparative predominance of short vibrations. The American scrape (Illustrations 64 (Ledet), 53d (Ledet), and 57f (Sprenkle)) has a slightly shorter tip, a little heavier heart, and the bark is taken off the back, allowing the lower overtones to fill in and enrich the tone.

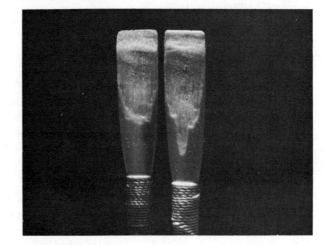

ILLUSTRATION 64

The amount of wood left in the lay or heart is a tempering influence on both the tip and the back. Too much or too little wood left in the heart area will cancel the effectiveness of the tip or the back. When the correct amount of wood is left in the heart to balance the tip and back, the tone will contain a very desirable core. The correct tip will make the reed responsive, giving ring and life to the sound, and the correct back will fill in the low partials, resulting in a rich quality. It should be remembered that the guide for balancing is that the tip should be thin to start with.

Following are some standard methods of adjusting the quality of a reed, using the above principles of short and long vibrations as a guide. The reed should be tried often and scraping should be stopped before the "point of no worthwhile return." To make a tone quality darker:

1. Lengthen the sides of the lay, especially in the corners near where it joins the back.

2. Scrape wood from the hump to free the vibrations into the back.

3. Scrape wood from the back. This can be done until just before F' or $F\sharp'$ become unstable

when the reed is played.

Occasionally, one finds that scraping wood off the reed will not remedy a particular situation and that the wood should have been left on. For example, if one has taken too much wood from the heart it is sometimes possible to trim the tip of the reed and remake the lay, moving it farther back on the cane. This, in effect or by comparison, adds more thickness of cane to the heart. It also makes the reed higher in pitch and adds resistance. To make a *brighter* quality:

1. Take less wood from the back.
2. Take more wood from the heart.
3. Make the tip longer.

The five main characteristics of a reed are so closely interrelated that it is almost impossible to adjust one of them without affecting one or more of the others. If the affected characteristics are changed for the better, then it is good. If they are changed for the worse, they may have to be adjusted a bit themselves. For example, if the *opening* is changed, the resistance, response, pitch, dynamic range, and playing quality can be affected. If the *resistance* is changed, the response, quality, and dynamic range can be affected. If the *pitch level* is altered, so, too, is the intonation of the oboe within itself. Sometimes the quality, response, and dynamic range are also affected.

Therefore, the process of reed adjustment is a compensation for strong or weak points by balancing the five characteristics to the point where they complement each other. The adjustment process may be a continuous one throughout the life of the reed, because some pieces of cane never become completely set. They usually need a bit of touching up as time goes on. The reedmaker should expect to adjust and "play in" a reed for several days after it is made before it will appear to operate at peak efficiency. Some will be nursed along and become good reeds only after a time. Some reeds play well early in their lives. Others will be mediocre, and then, in a blaze of artistic glory, will be excellent reeds for a brief hour, and then return to their mediocrity. Some are split in the scraping process while others are cut off the staple to be replaced by better pieces of cane. When the acid in an oboist's saliva takes its toll or the fibers have been broken down by tonguing and vibrations of many notes, any further adjustment would reach the point of diminishing returns. The reed is then worn out and should be cut off the staple. The staple should be scrubbed out, another piece of cane bound on, and another reed scraped.

The standard tools for oboe reedmaking, along with the gouging, shaping, binding, scraping, and adjusting processes have now been presented. All of these elements are necessary in any style of reedmaking. The "finished" reed illustrations in the text are examples of one generally-accepted American style which is recommended to the beginner as a good, usable, proven reed style. A professional oboist makes his particular type of reed because of his individual method of tone production (breathing, embouchure, etc.), particular instrument, teachers, and aural concept. The student, having no basis in experience for his judgment, should have a definite model toward which to work. After he has achieved some success and consistency in a style of reedmaking it is very simple for him to deviate from the original idea in order to more closely suit his individual needs and desires.

It is heartily recommended that students develop a strong curiosity regarding the visual aspects of all oboe reeds in relation to the actual sound produced, and to constantly hear and evaluate professional oboists both in person and on recordings. This developing of discrimination in oboe sound will guide the player's reed knife in the years to come. When the reed *complements* rather than *inhibits* the other links in the chain (tone production, embouchure, instrument, etc.), it will contribute its important part to performance.